Building Blocks
vSphere 6.0 and vCenter 6.0

Tom Burge
Calvin Kohler-Katz

CompuTom, Inc.
Dallas, Texas
2016

CompuTom, Inc.
https://www.computom.com/
info@computom.com

Ordering Information:

Available exclusively on the Amazon Kindle Store.

Other Books Coming Soon

Cisco UCS 3.0 Install and Configuration
Cisco UCS Central Install and Configuration
HP Bladecenter c7000 Gen8/9 Install and Configuration
Microsoft Active Directory and Services + Azure AD
Microsoft Exchange 2013/2016 Install and Upgrade
Microsoft Identity Manager 2016
Microsoft Skype for Business 2015
Microsoft System Center Configuration Manager
Microsoft System Center Orchestrator
Microsoft System Center Operations Manager
Microsoft System Center Service Manager
Microsoft System Center Virtual Machine Manager and Hyper-V
Microsoft SQL Server 2014/2016 Install with AlwaysOn Availability Groups
VMware Horizon 7 + Install and Configuration
VMware Site Recovery Manager Install and Configuration
VMware vRealize Operations Manager

Table of Contents

Introduction

Why this book? Well like most people I love to learn, but I have a hard time finding good thorough and comprehensive guides on how to set things up from the get go. I live by the philosophy of learn by doing so in the spirit of that, I wanted to create a guide for anyone to be able to use to set up a vSphere environment from the ground up.

I have bought a lot of books and eBooks in my time and I love to read, but when it comes to reading about performing tasks there is a lot lacking. Most books I find deal with the "fluff" (not to say the fluff isn't necessary) around the products and I find myself having dig out the specific steps. Sometimes the books or blogs have steps 1-5 and 8-10, but they glossed over some really important stuff in 6-7. I wanted to demystify the technology for everyone.

My goal here is to provide a structured how-to following current validated design principles. A lot of books and blogs are great when it comes to setting up a test lab, but production builds are a different story. Many companies tend to rely on professional services from vendors or value added resellers (I call them stress added resellers). I want anyone, from a help desk level agent to a senior systems administrator, to be able to pick up this book and perform all of the tasks without asking "Well...what about this? What do I do here?".

This is our first book and we will be creating many more. We welcome all feedback that can contribute to our process and presentation. Please feel free to email us at info@computom.com. Use the book title as the subject line and include your name if you wish to be credited for your input if we decide to incorporate it.

Server names and IPs may be censored for security's sake.

In keeping with my no fluff policy, let's begin.

Obtain Media and License Keys

Before you are able to obtain any media or license keys you will need to make an account with VMware.

Use this link: https://my.vmware.com/web/vmware/registration

Once you go through the whole process and validate your email and blah blah blah, you will be able to access downloads, trials and all that jazz. If your company already has licenses and they are connected to your account, you will be able to head right on into the downloads. Navigating the VMware downloads section can be challenging and they definitely need to overhaul it.

Here is what the My VMware user page looks like:

You can click on View & Download Products to head to the downloads or click Manage License Keys to view any licenses you might have.

If you have no license keys, use this link: https://www.vmware.com/try-vmware

The link should list all the products that are available for evaluation licenses. This is a pretty comprehensive list so if you don't see something on here then just contact your VMware account executive and they can get you hooked up.

Once you have evaluation licenses, you may want to keep track of them. Hover over Products and click on My Evaluations. This will take you to the evaluation center where you can keep track of any current evaluations you have open.

We will be using VMware ESXi 6.0 U2 for this book.

Here is what the download page for VMware ESXi 6.0 U2 looks like:

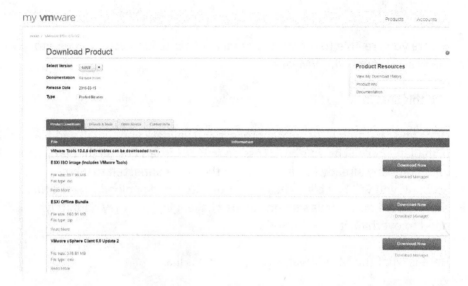

In the Product Downloads table, you will see the basic ISO images, offline bundles (don't worry I'll explain later) and things like the client. Here is where you will decide what is right for you.

If you have:

A) White box machine

   Download the ESXi ISO image (Includes VMware Tools)

B) Branded server like HP, Dell or a Cisco

   Click on the Custom ISOs tab

Click Go To Downloads on the brand of machine that you have.

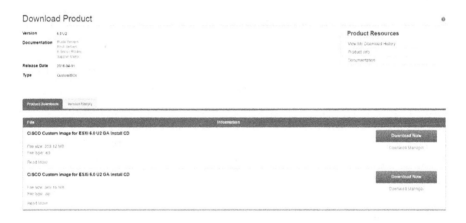

Click Download Now on the File Type: iso

Next head back to the Product Downloads page.

You will want to download VMware vSphere Client 6.0 Update 2 next just as you did on ESXi.

The next thing you will want to pick up is VMware vCenter Server 6.0 U2.

Here is what the VMware vCenter Server 6.0 U2 download page looks like:

You will see three options on this page and this is where you need to make a decision.

In the past, VCSA had some scalability issues, but this has since been corrected, so basically the decision comes down to ease of management and money.

With the VCSA, you will not need to buy any Windows Server or SQL Server licenses for vCenter. You will need Windows Server and SQL Server licenses for Update Manager.

With the vCenter for Windows, you will need Windows Server and SQL Server licenses. The SQL Server can be used for both vCenter and Update Manager so they will not need to be separate.

We will provide guides on how to set up both systems, but my suggestion is to go the vCenter for Windows route since you will need it for Update Manager anyway.

At this time, you should have three things:

VMware ESXi 6.0 U2
VMware vCenter Server 6.0 U2
VMware vSphere Client 6.0 Update 2

Moving on!

Decide Install Type

So there are two types of installations to be concerned with: Manual (Media) and Scripted (Also from Media)

The Manual install is a straight install by using a CD or USB drive with the installation media following the prompts. The ESXi install is super simple and straight forward, however... if you have to do this on 76 hosts in a couple of days then your colleagues might find you crying in the corner of the datacenter one day.

So I present to you scripted installation. The scripted installation is super simple. You use a preconfigured script to answer all of the prompts for you and everything completes with no input. The good thing about the script is that you can use one of three locations to hold your scripts: CD, USB, or Network (do this).

There are two other ways to install, but I'm not going to get into them with this guide. We might do a blog post about them. If we decide to, it will be listed in the appendix or in a linked blog post.

We will perform both a manual ESXi install and a scripted installation.

On to the next section!

Decide Install Location

In this section, we will talk about the three different places that you can install ESXi. You may have heard about AutoDeploy, but go ahead and forget about that for now.

We have three (or two?) options for installing ESXi: Local Disk, Local SD card/USB, and Boot from SAN.

Local disk is good, but expensive. You can maintain scratch space and syslogs on these but overall ESXi is only a couple hundred megabytes. This is kind of overkill.

Local USB/SD cards are great. USB/SD cards are super cheap and pretty much every single vendor out there supports them. USB/SD cards have a negative on the scratch/syslog situation, but that's ok because we are going to talk about redirecting them anyway since that is a common practice.

Boot from SAN is straight up overkill, BUT unless you have a major storage failure, you can do a quick swap out of hardware and have another host ready as soon as you rack it without having to configure RAID groups and all that jazz for the other two options.

My personal preference and the most widespread situation is the USB/SD card installation. I won't cover Boot from SAN, but it is possible.

We're done with this section.

Decide Network Information

This is a very important planning section and this can widely vary between organizations. There are two major topics in the networking field (really three, but that comes later). They are VLANs and Addressing Type (IPv4 and IPv6).

Almost any organization more than 20 people will have VLANs, but what you need to be concerned with is trunking. Host ports are trunked ports. That means they can see multiple networks at one time (think virtual machines). Every VLAN that will belong to the host (vMotion, Virtual Machines, Host Management, etc.) will need to be trunked to the network ports that your hosts are using. Your network team/individual should be able to fill you in on all of the details with what you need.

Second is Addressing. IPv4 or IPv6. Well that is not even a question. Use IPv4 and turn off IPv6. We are private organizations using private networks. That is what the 10.0.0.0/8, 172.16.0.0/12, and 192.168.0.0/16 are used for. Forgive me if I did not get those ranges correct. Every organization I have been part of has used the 10.x.x.x or 172.x.x.x networks for the internal networking. I believe there is some supportability issues with some VMware products for IPv6 as well. Just go with IPv4 and make your life a whole lot easier.

At the end of this section, you should have the following information for your install:

Hostname (FQDN)
Static IP (Don't use DHCP)
Net mask
Gateway
VLAN (if applicable)
Two DNS Servers

Another thing to note is something called LACP or LAGs. This is network load balancing for using network adapters in an Active/Active state instead of the Active/Standby. LACP/LAG is always preferable because you will have twice the throughput as long as you are in a healthy state. Your network team/individual will be able to fill you in and I will show you where to configure it later.

At some point we will get to the good stuff, but we have to take care of the boring stuff first.

Prepare Hardware and Storage

I don't really have anything for you here. There is no way for me to be comprehensive about setting up different servers and storage platforms. I will be providing comprehensive guides on standing up and configuring HP and Cisco Blades. Transitioning from traditional rack mount servers to blades is a big change for the datacenter. People are also talking about buzz words like hyper-converged. I am more of a traditionalist and I like building my own solutions. I am an engineer at heart and having someone hand me a fully set up solution makes me feel lazy. I like the nitty gritty details and the super flexibility that the traditional rack/blade solutions can give. Companies like VCE and Nutanix are hot commodities, but just not my cup of tea.

This section was really looking empty so I just wanted to give my two cents.

Prep your stuff and get ready to go!

Install ESXi (Manual Install)

1. Insert your media into the server (CD or USB mounted ISO).

2. Boot your server and select the boot options.

3. Select the device you are using to install.

4. When the device boots you will see the following screen:

5. Wait or hit Enter.

6. Wait or hit Enter.

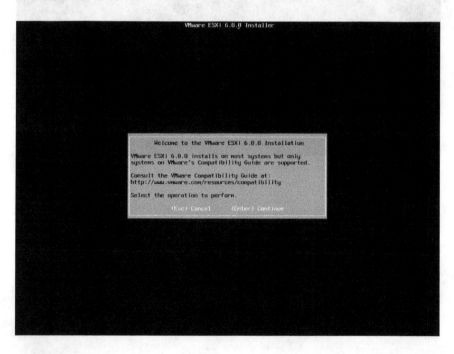

7. Hit Enter.

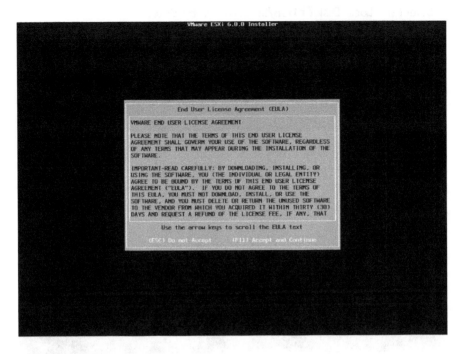

8. Read the EULA (LOL) and hit F11.

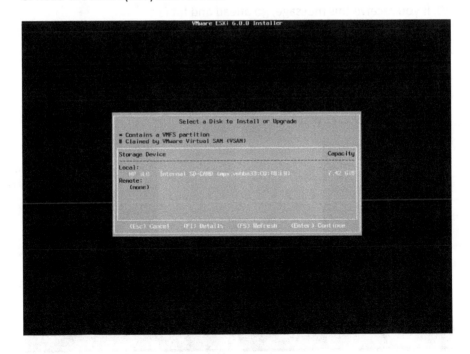

9. Select the Local Disk or USB/SD card and hit Enter.

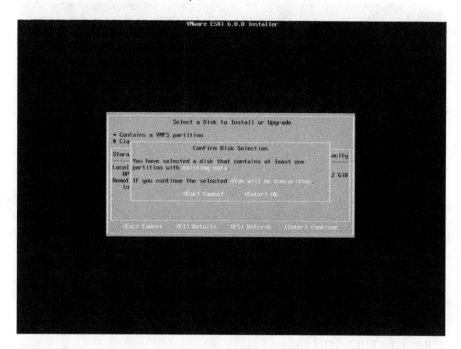

10. If you receive this message, go ahead and hit Enter.

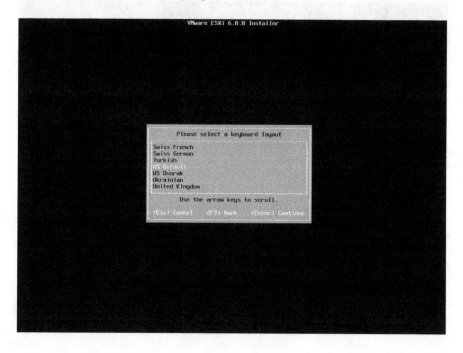

11. Select your Keyboard Layout.

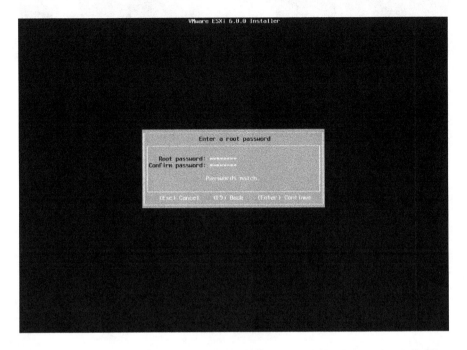

12. Enter the root password you would like twice and hit Enter.

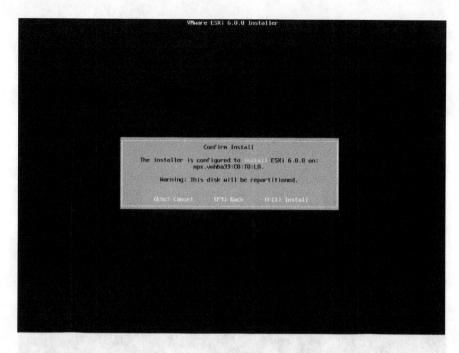

13. Hit F11 if you are sure and the drive will be partitioned and ESXi will be installed.

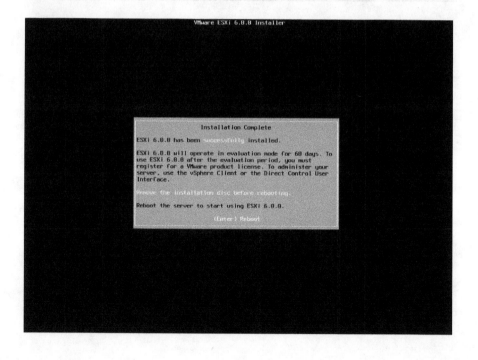

14. Reboot! You're done!

Install ESXi (Scripted Install)

For the scripted install of ESXi, we will need to setup our script and place it in a good location. I am using HTTP for my scripts so that is the scenario that we will run through.

First make a text file and call it host1.cfg. Use the following block of text for the script:

```
# Sample scripted installation file
#
# Accept EULA
vmaccepteula
# Set root password
rootpw password
# Cleans the Partition
cleanpart --firstdisk=usb
# Install on local disk overwriting any existing VMFS datastore
install --firstdisk=usb --overwritevmfs
# Network configuration
network --bootproto=static --device=vmnic0 --ip=172.26.107.120 --
netmask=255.255.255.0 --gateway=172.26.107.1 --
nameserver=172.26.94.11 --hostname=host1.test.tom --vlanid=612 --
addvmportgroup=1
# Reboot after installation completed
reboot
```

This is a basic script and it will get the job done. There is a lot more options and they are documented on the VMware Documentation page.

When you are making this script, try and use Notepad++.

Make sure the EOL Conversion is set to UNIX.
Make sure the Encoding is set to UTF-8.

Otherwise your script will show up with some unknown character errors. After the script is complete and copied to a web server, follow these steps.

1. Insert your media into the server (CD or USB mounted ISO).

2. Boot your server and select the boot options.

3. Select the device you are using to install.

Here is the first screen you will see:

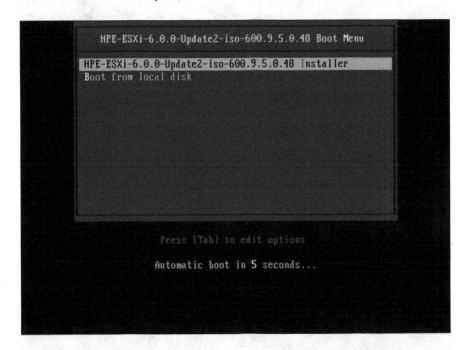

4. You can hit Enter or wait for the timer.

5. Hold Shift + O to trigger the boot options.

6. On this line I have shown in the screenshot a sample configuration line.

Modify the following example and replace it with your information and hit Enter.

runweasel ks=http://<webserver-ip>/configs/host1.cfg ip=<host-ip> netmask=255.255.255.0 gateway=<gateway-ip> nameserver=<dns-ip> vlanid=0

The installer will load and you will see this screen next that confirms whether your script is working:

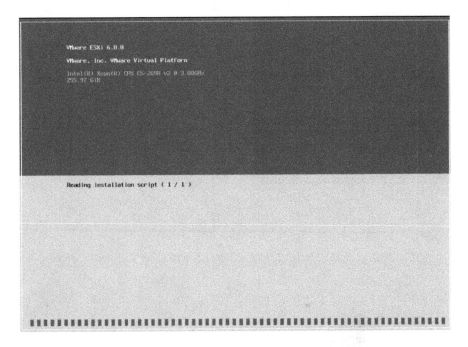

After a little while, the install will finish and reboot the server.

You should receive this screen when it is complete:

```
VMware ESXi 6.0.0 (VMKernel Release Build 3620759)

HP ProLiant BL460c Gen8

2 x Intel(R) Xeon(R) CPU E5-2690 v2 @ 3.00GHz
256 GiB Memory




Download tools to manage this host from:
http://host1/
http://█████████/ (STATIC)
http://[fe80::2c81:efff:fe30:f41/ (STATIC)




<F2> Customize System/View Logs                            <F12> Shut Down/Restart
```

Wooo! Scripted install complete!

Configure ESXi (DCUI)

After the install, your server rebooted and now you are at the DCUI (Direct Console User Interface). This is where you can do some basic configuration to get your system online.

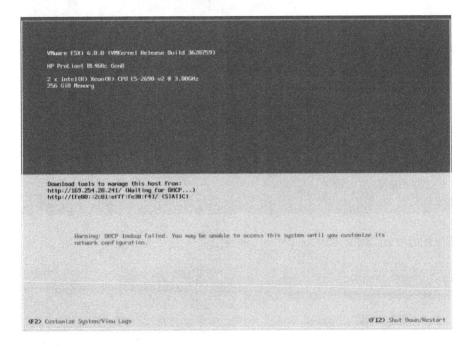

If you did a scripted install, the script took care of all of this stuff. Head on over to the next section or follow along to validate the script.

1. Hit F2.

2. Enter the root password and hit Enter.

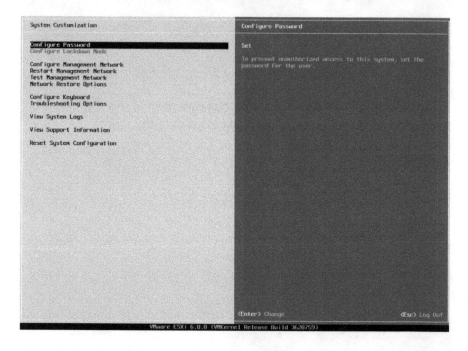

This is the DCUI configuration menu. Most of the time, you will not use this.

3. Use the arrow keys and move down to Configure Management Network.

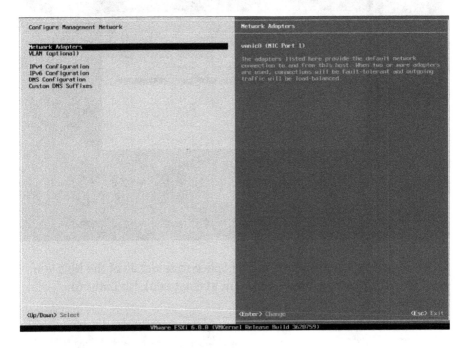

The management network is how ESXi communicates on the network.

4. Hit Enter to select Network Adapters.

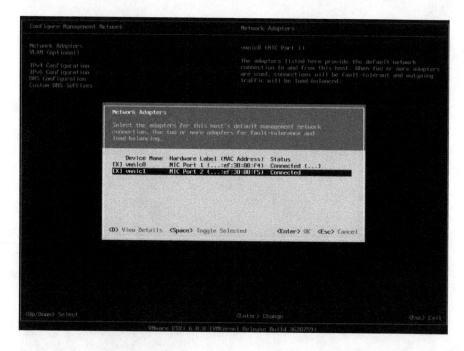

5. Use the arrow keys to move and hit Space to select all of the NICs you want to use for management (you want at least two). Hit Enter to confirm.

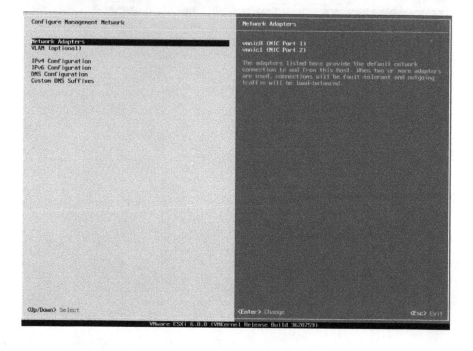

In the right panel, you will now see the selected network adapters for the management network.

6. Arrow down to VLAN (optional) and hit Enter.

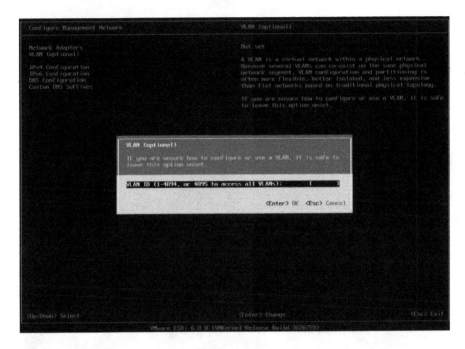

This is only applicable if you use VLANs in your environment.

7. Enter the VLAN for the Management Network that you defined in the pre-requisites earlier. Hit Enter.

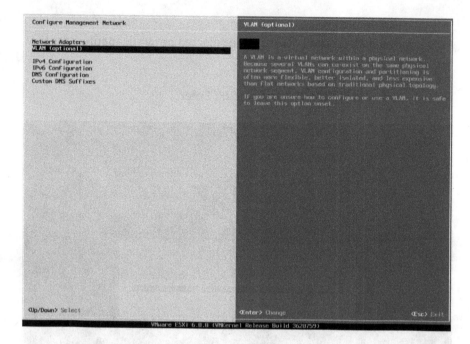

In the right panel, you will now see your VLAN ID.

8. Arrow down to IPv4 Configuration and Hit Enter.

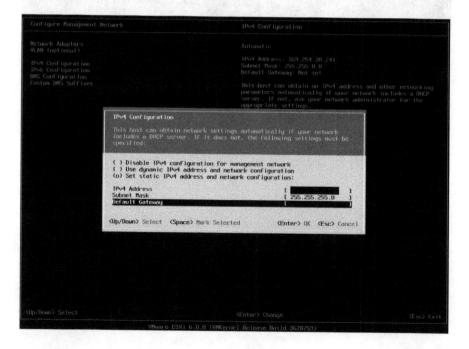

9. Arrow down to Set Static IPv4 and hit Space. Enter the IPv4 address, subnet mask, and gateway. Hit Enter.

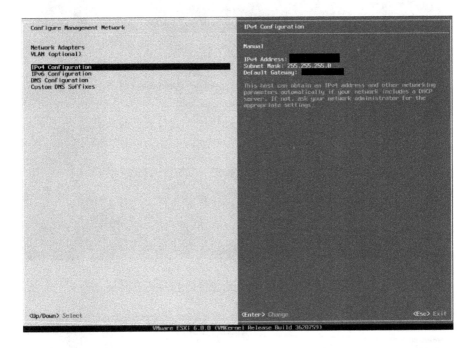

In the right panel, you will see your address, subnet mask, and gateway now configured.

10. Arrow down to IPv6 Configuration and Hit Enter.

11. Arrow up to Disable IPv6 and hit Space. Hit Enter to confirm.

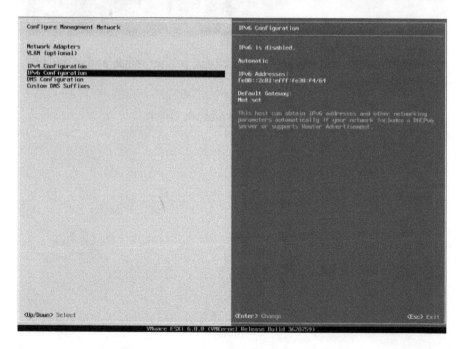

In the right panel, IPv6 will now say it is disabled.

12. Arrow down to DNS Configuration and hit Enter.

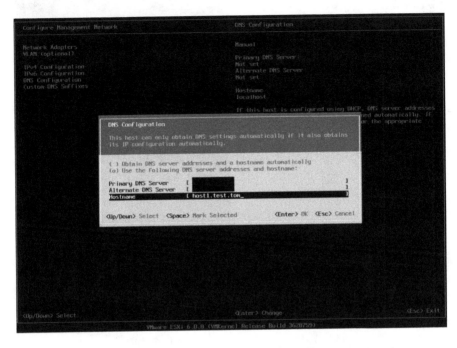

13. Enter the DNS servers and the hostname you determined in the pre-requisites then hit Enter.

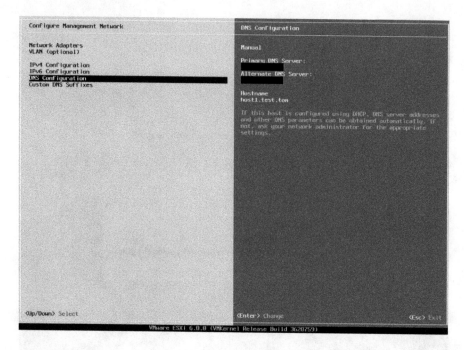

In the right panel, you will now see your DNS servers and hostname configured.

14. Arrow down to Custom DNS Suffixes and hit Enter.

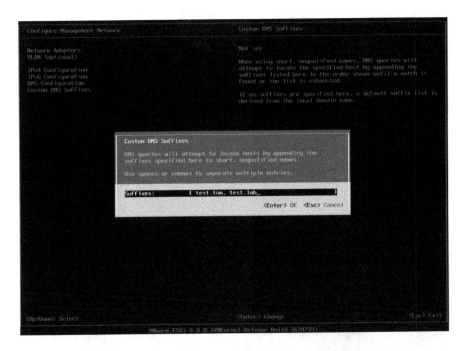

15. Enter all of the DNS suffixes in use for your network with commas or spaces and hit Enter.

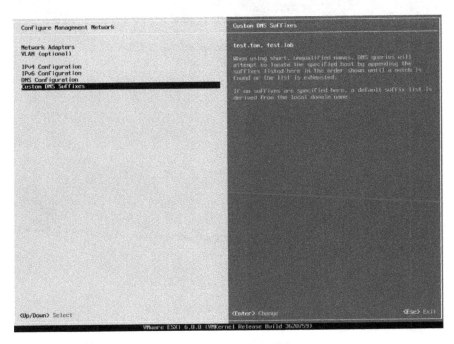

In the right panel, you will see your DNS suffixes listed.

16. Hit Escape.

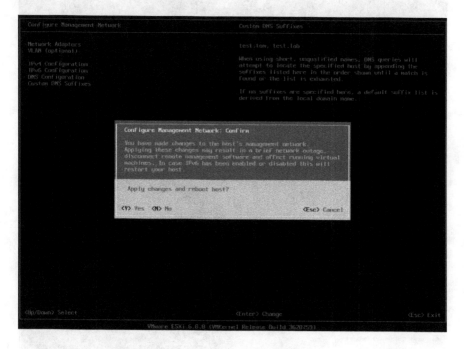

17. Hit Y to accept the changes you have made and reboot.

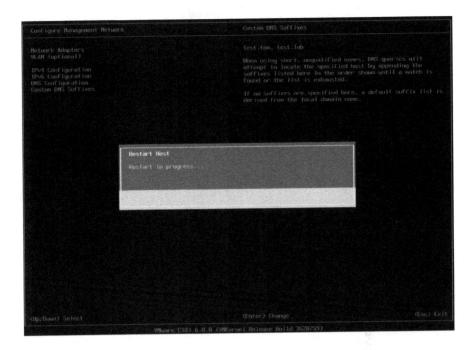

The host will now reboot and it should come back up to the following screen.

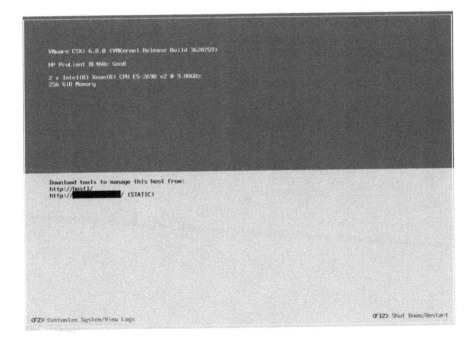

Congrats! You are now ready to configure ESXi with the vSphere Client!

Configure ESXi (vSphere Client)

In this section, we will use the full client to finish configuring the new host that we have installed. This is where you will begin from a scripted installation. This also occurs after the DCUI configuration for a manual installation.

Before we begin, you will want to make sure to install the vSphere client. After that has complete, go ahead and follow the steps.

1. Start the vSphere Client.

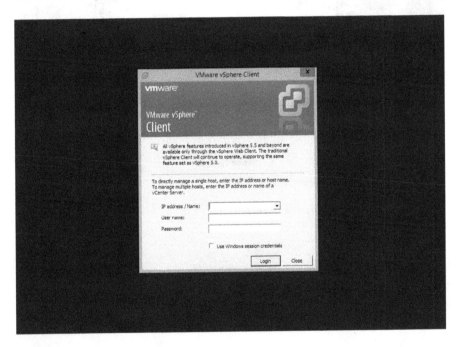

2. Enter the IP address/DNS name of the host, root, and the root password that you assigned. Click Login.

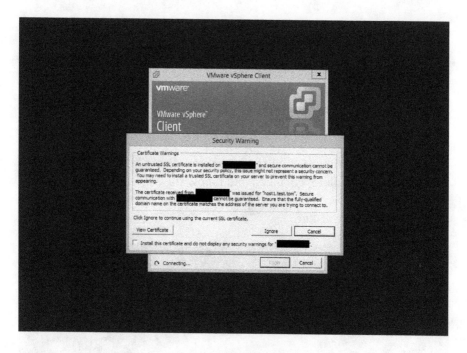

3. You will receive a certification warning. Click Ignore to continue.

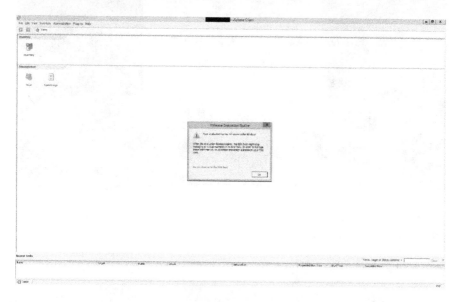

4. You will receive an evaluation notice because your host is not licensed. You will have 60 days to enter a key or it will downgrade to the free version. Click OK to continue.

On this screen is the basic information for the host. As you can tell, there is not a lot here.

5. Click Inventory.

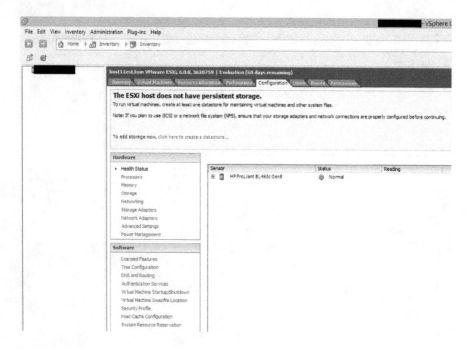

Oh no! No persistent storage. You will always receive this error when using a USB/SD card. If you are using local hard drives, you will not receive this message. The host recognizes that the attached USB/SD card is not a real disk and wants you to send your scratch and logs to a persistent file. We will get to that later.

6. If the client did not default to the configuration tab, click Configuration now.

You will see a split pane with two sections called Hardware and Software. These are where the host configuration settings are located and we will go through them all. You should be defaulted to the Health Status screen. If not already there, select Health Status.

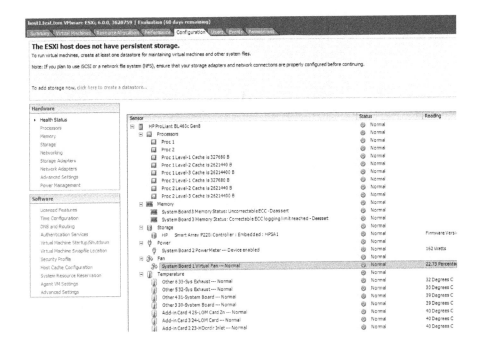

If you used a custom ISO then you should have your manufacturer's agents embedded to show detailed hardware information. As you can see, We are using a HP BL460c Gen8 blade.

7. Click the + to browse through this information.

8. Next, select Processors.

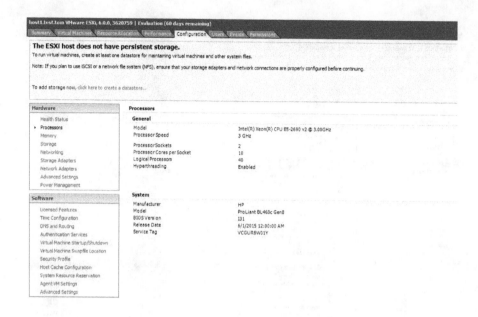

Here you can see specific information about your processor like sockets, cores, etc. If you have a custom image, you can see the system information below the processor information.

9. Select Memory.

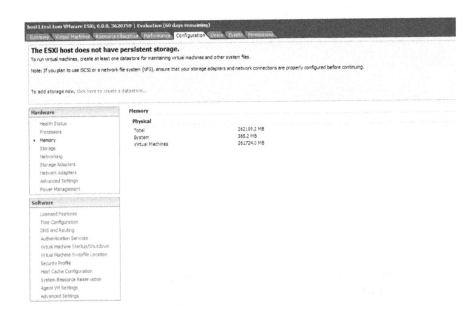

Same deal here. You can see information about memory capacity and usage. Very basic information.

10. Select Storage.

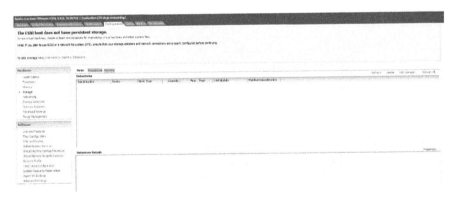

On this screen, you can see any datastores or devices you have. You can also refresh the view, add storage, and rescan the host bus adapters. We will come back to this later on.

11. Select Networking.

Here is where we will check your network configuration and configure some more stuff.

12. Click Properties next to vSwitch0.

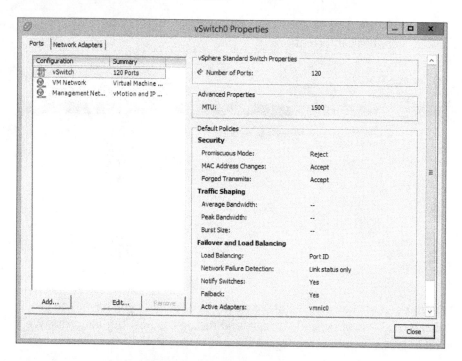

This shows the basic properties of the network switch and allows you to add/remove port groups, change network adapter settings, etc.

13. Click Network Adapters.

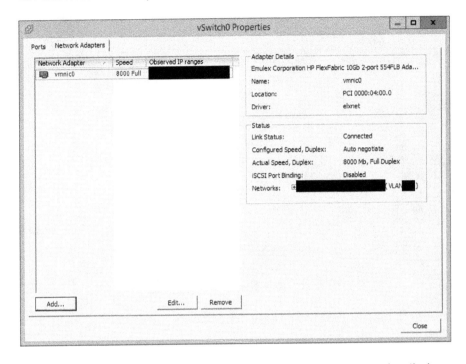

Here you can see your network adapters and view some more detailed information about them. As you can see, I only have one

14. Click Add.

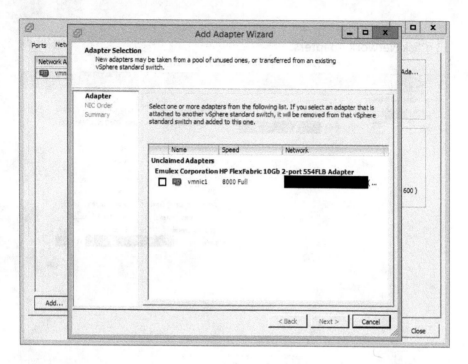

15. Check the box next to any network adapters you want to add and click Next.

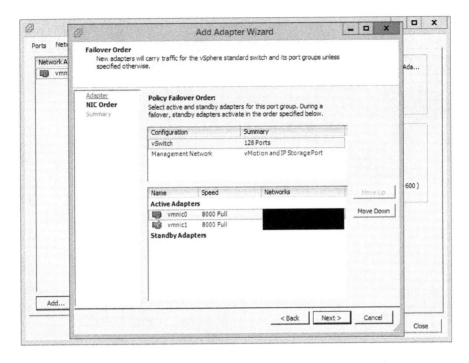

In this box, you can move a network adapter to be standby if you want. I use an active/active configuration so I will leave it as is.

16. Click Next.

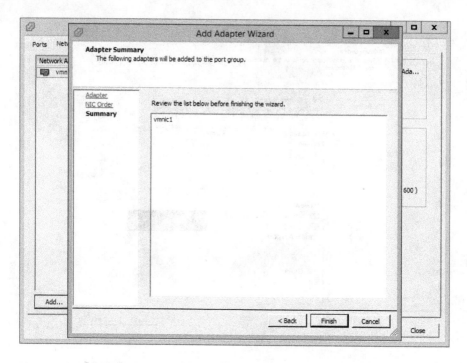

This screen will give a list of the network adapters you are adding.

17. Click Finish.

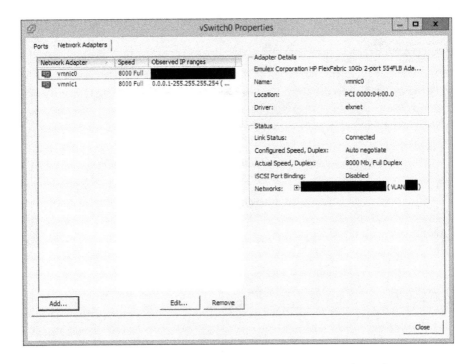

You will return to the main screen and see now that you have however many network adapters you selected. I have two.

18. Click Ports to return to the original window.

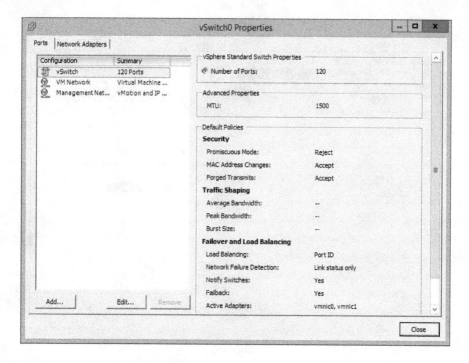

19. Select vSwitch and click Edit.

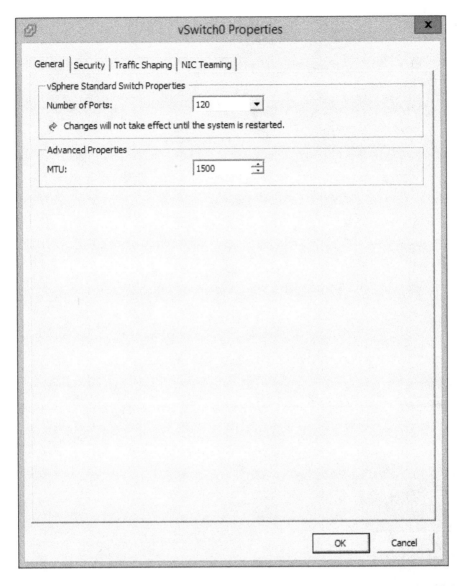

Here is the properties window of the vSwitch. You can configure top level settings that can filter down to port groups and network adapters. I'm just going to leave the defaults since I don't intend on using a Standard Switch for my end state.

20. Click Security.

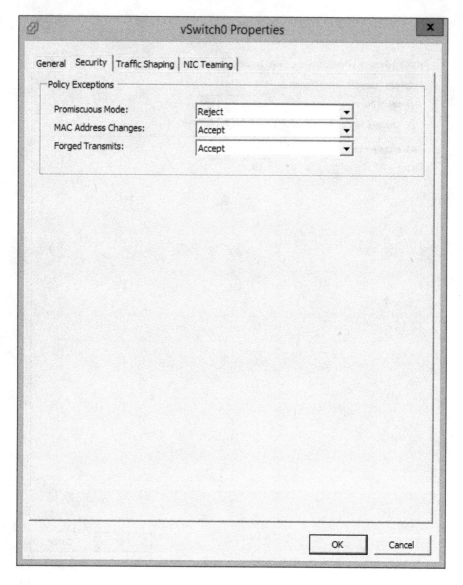

Here are the default security settings for the vSwitch. Just leave the
defaults for now.

21. Click Traffic Shaping.

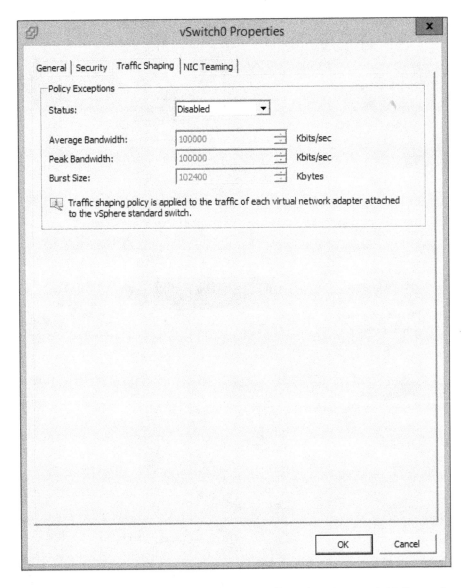

Traffic shaping is disabled by default. We will get into Network IO Control and Traffic Shaping later.

22. Click NIC Teaming

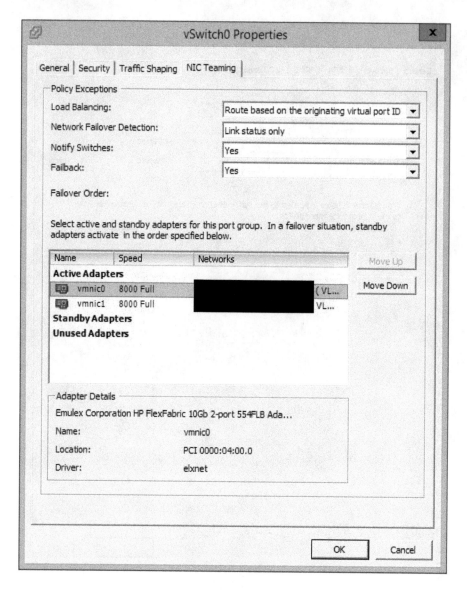

On this tab, you can see the network adapter policies. If you select a network adapter you can see the driver and bus ID for it as well. We won't change anything here for now.

23. Click OK.

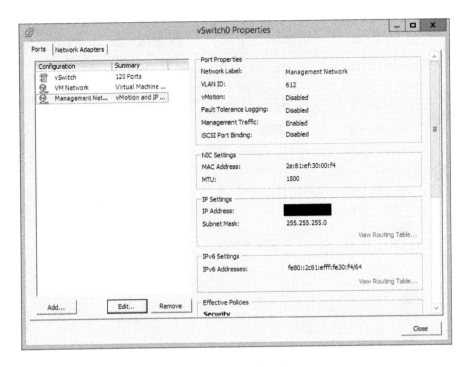

24. Select Management Network and Click Edit.

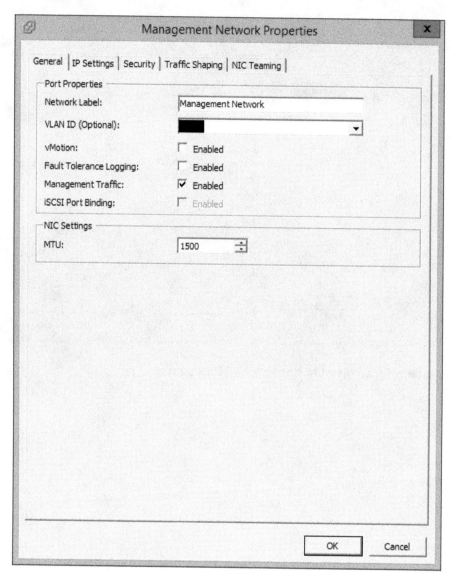

You will see some similar settings from the higher vSwitch along with additional settings. This is the management network vmkernel port group. VMKernel port groups are different than VM Network port groups because they have additional management options that virtual machines do not need.

Here you change the label of the port group, VLAN ID, management traffic type and the MTU. Leave everything default for now.

25. Click IP Settings.

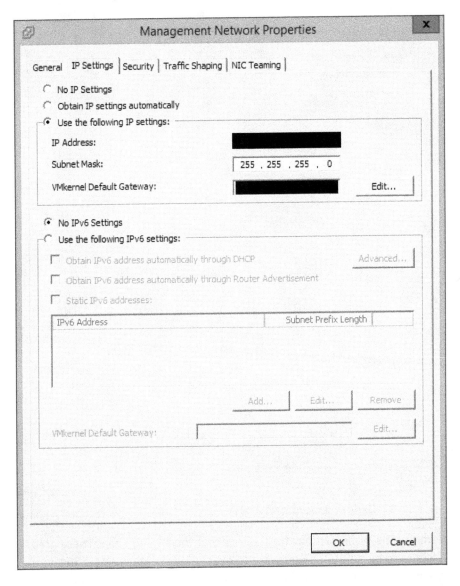

Here you can verify that the IP settings are correct.

26. Click Security.

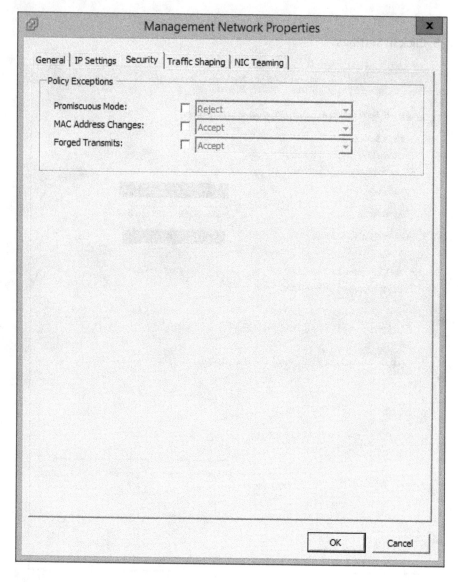

Here are the same settings for security that the vSwitch had. These are all unchecked by default. If you want to override a switch level setting, you would check the box and change the setting. I don't need to change anything right now so I will leave the defaults.

27. Click Traffic Shaping.

General | IP Settings | Security | Traffic Shaping | NIC Teaming

Policy Exceptions

To override a policy defined by the switch, check the box below.

Status: ☐ Disabled ▾

Average Bandwidth: 100000   Kbits/sec

Peak Bandwidth: 100000   Kbits/sec

Burst Size: 102400   Kbytes

ℹ Traffic shaping policy is applied to the traffic of each virtual network adapter attached to the port group.

OK   Cancel

Same deal as before. These settings are for exceptions to the default vSwitch policies.

28. Click NIC Teaming.

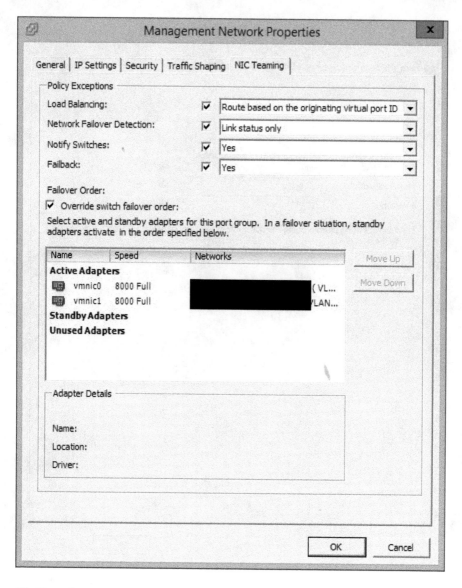

29. Now that we are done here, click OK.

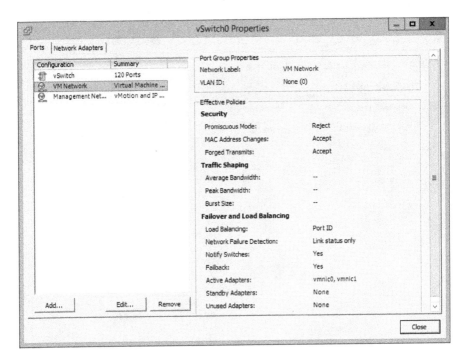

30. Select VM Network and click Edit.

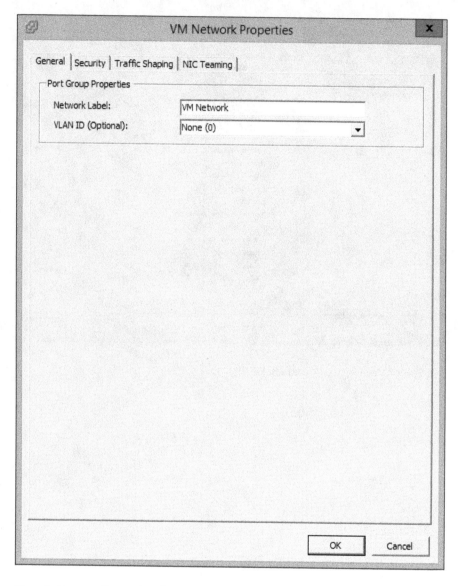

Here is the configuration for the virtual machine port group. Here you can set the label for the network and the VLAN ID.

31. Set the VLAN ID for this network to match the one you will use for virtual machines. Click OK.

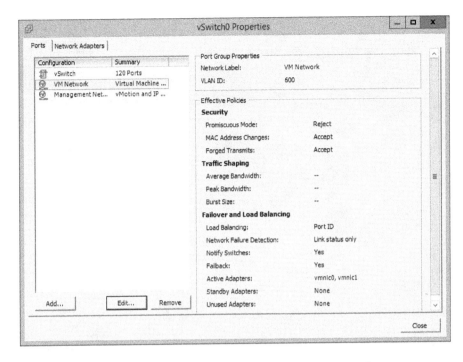

We have one more thing to do to finish up the network configuration. Do not use your management VMkernel for vMotion traffic. Make a separate VMkernel port group for vMotion. Now time to add vMotion!

32. Click Add.

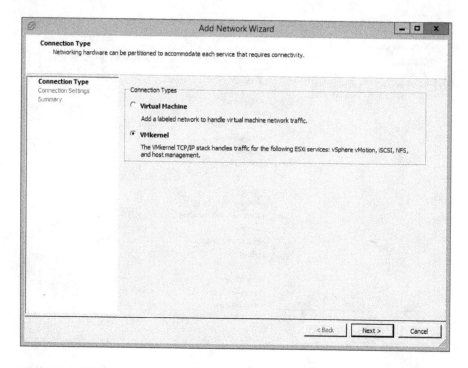

33. Select VMKernel and click Next.

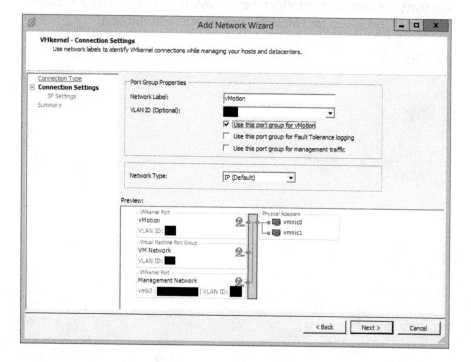

34. Label the new port group, enter a VLAN ID, check the vMotion checkbox and click Next.

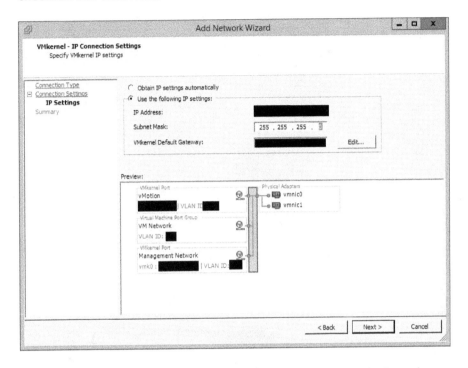

Every VMKernel adapter needs an IP address. Management is the only one that needs a DNS name.

35. Enter the IP information for this adapter. Click Next.

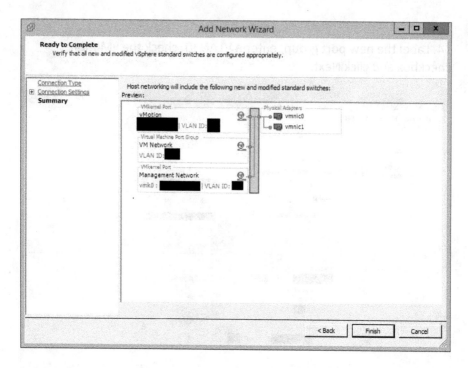

36. Review the information and click Finish.

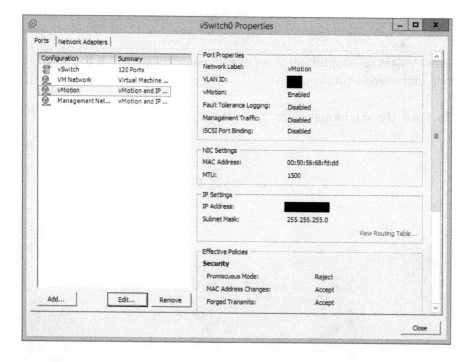

Now you have separate vMotion and Management adapters!

37. Click Close.

Here you can validate that it added to the vSwitch and that you are good to go!

We are going to skip over storage adapters for now.

38. Click Network Adapters.

Here you can see information about all of the network adapters available in the system.

39. Select Power Management.

This is very important. Make sure High Performance is selected. As you can see mine is not.

40. Click Properties.

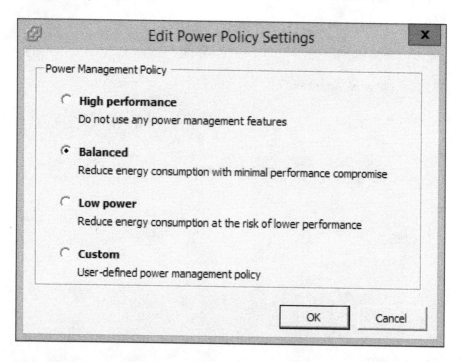

41. Click the radio button on High Performance and click OK.

42. Click Refresh and make sure that it now says High Performance.

***Side note: Check your BIOS for power settings as well. Some servers have performance profiles that can be set in the BIOS that work outside the VMware settings.

43. Click Licensed Features.

Here you can see all of the features available in ESXi. Once you apply a license key, you may see less features depending on the version you selected. I will apply a license once vCenter is deployed.

44. Click Time Configuration.

Time configuration is very important in ESXi. I don't really want to make a blog post about it, but make sure every single host in your environment has the NTP client configured and enabled. It is important all your hosts' clocks are in sync. You will have problems if they aren't.

45. Click Properties.

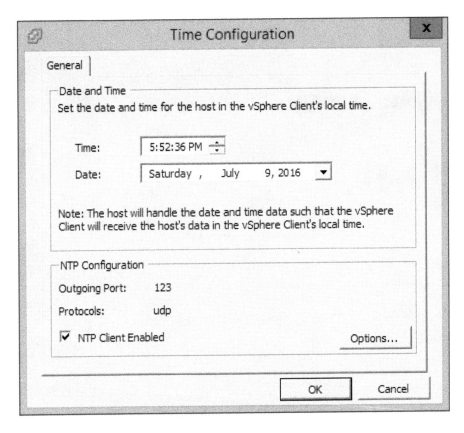

46. Check the box and click Options.

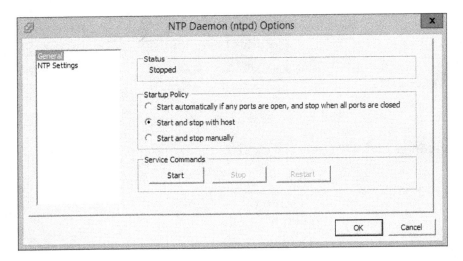

47. Select the radio button for start and stop with host. Click NTP Settings

on the left panel.

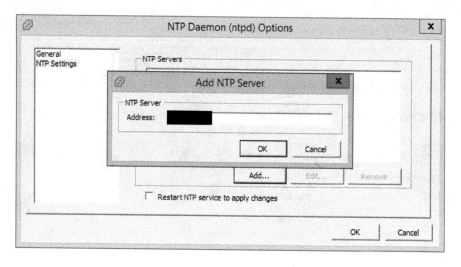

48. Click Add.

49. Enter your NTP Server and click OK.

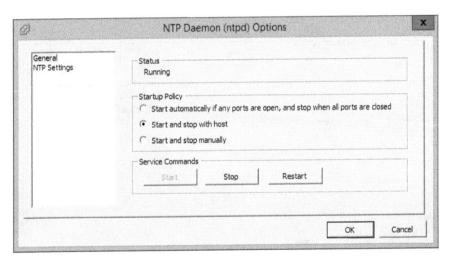

50. Check the box Restart NTP and click General in the left panel.

51. Click Start. If the radio button changes to manual, set it back to start and stop with host. Click OK.

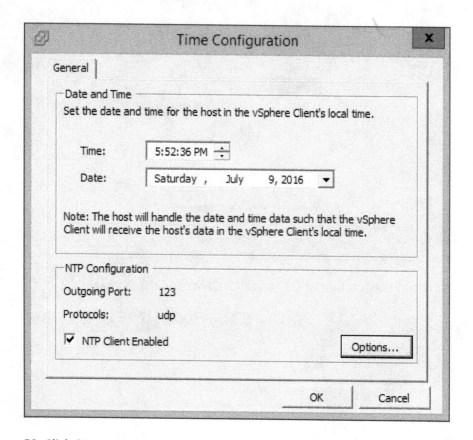

52. Click OK.

Your time and date should be accurate now. Click Refresh to update it if it is not.

53. Select DNS and Routing.

Here is where your DNS servers, FQDN and gateway are configured. Ensure that these are accurate.

54. Select Storage Adapters.

Here is the storage adapter configuration. On this screen, we can see the Fibre Channel Host Bus Adapters and any devices connected to them. Right now I don't have any LUNs zoned into this host. There is one additional thing we can do here and that is add iSCSI. I'm going to leave this for an appendix since it is a little bit involved.

55. Select Storage.

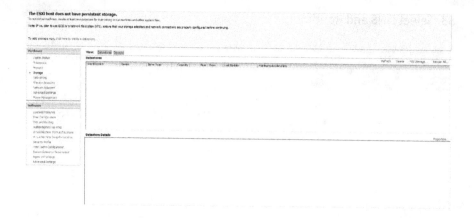

56. Click Add Storage. (This step is for NFS)

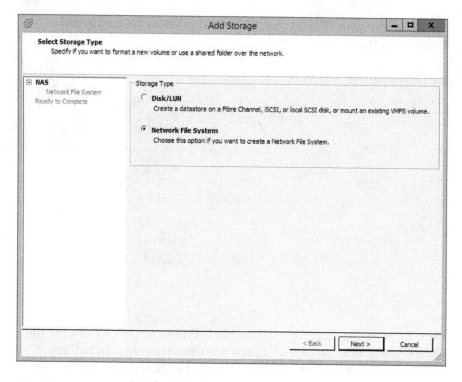

57. Select Network File System and click Next.

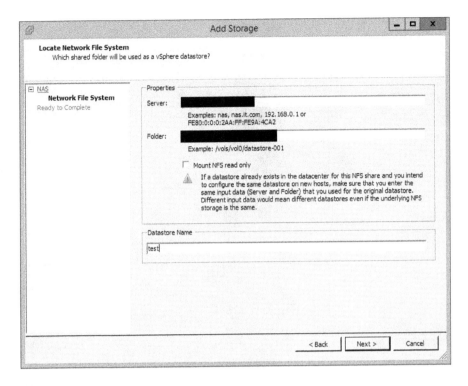

58. Enter the NFS server and the full path to the NFS export. Type a name for the datastore. Click Next.

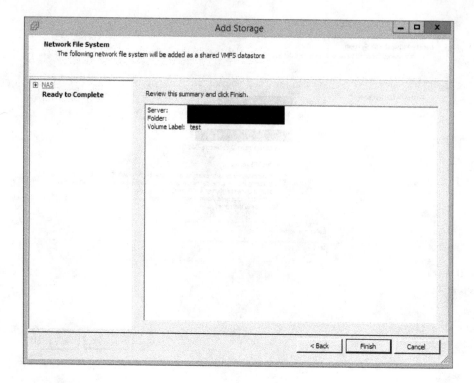

59. Click Finish.

Now you have created your first datastore!

60. Click Rescan All.

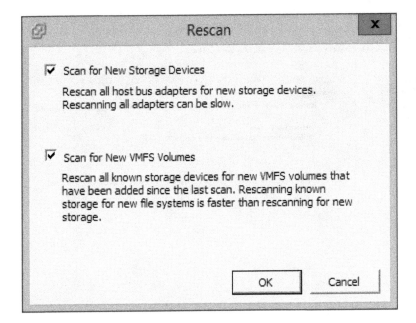

Rescan

☑ Scan for New Storage Devices

Rescan all host bus adapters for new storage devices.
Rescanning all adapters can be slow.

☑ Scan for New VMFS Volumes

Rescan all known storage devices for new VMFS volumes that
have been added since the last scan. Rescanning known
storage for new file systems is faster than rescanning for new
storage.

OK   Cancel

61. Click OK.

62. Click Add Storage. (This step is for Fibre Channel)

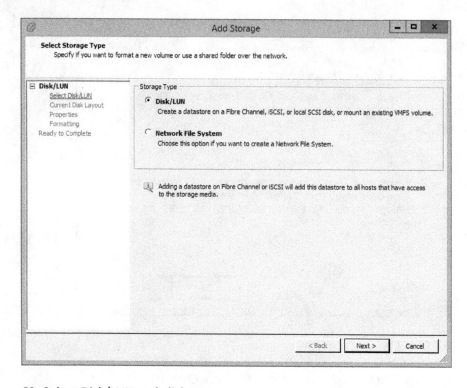

63. Select Disk/LUN and click Next.

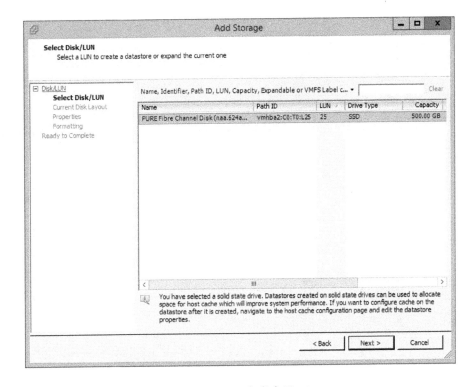

64. Select the LUN you want to use and click Next.

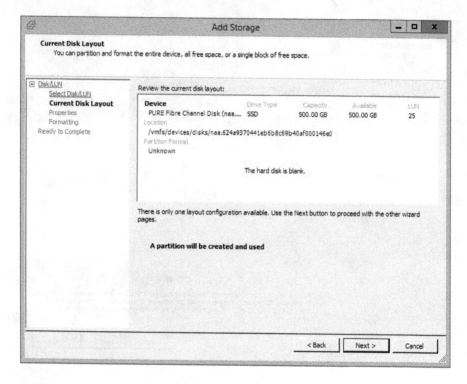

65. Review the information on this screen and click Next.

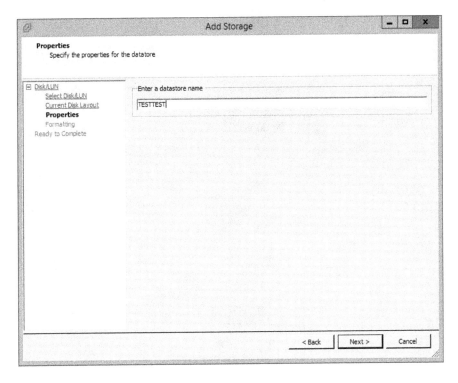

66. Enter a name for the datastore and click Next.

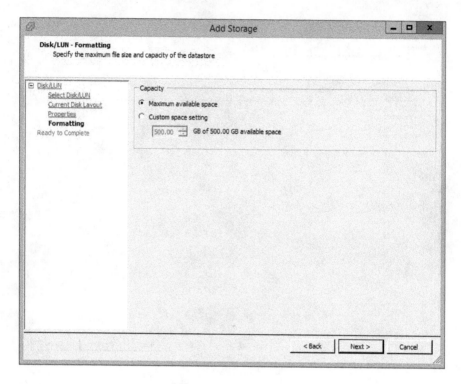

67. Make sure maximum available space is selected and click Next.

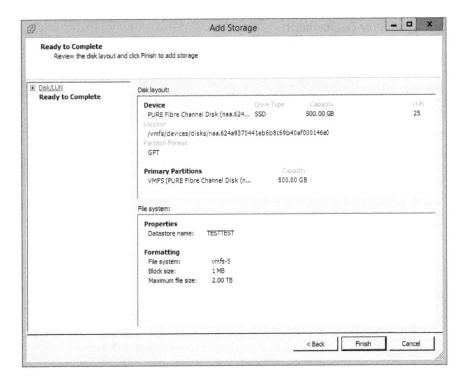

68. Review the information and click Finish.

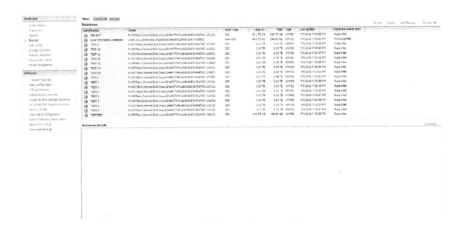

Woo! New Fibre Channel datastore added!

Repeat as necessary to add all the datastores you need.

This concludes the vSphere configuration section. Next up, we will be talking vCenter Deployment!

Deploy vCenter for Windows

In this section, we will be deploying vCenter for Windows. This is my personal preference for vCenter installations and it enables you to take advantage of the Enhanced Linked Mode. There is a few pre-requisites that you will need to take care of before installing and it requires a bit more maintenance than the vCenter Server Appliance does, but it is well worth it!

You will need the following software to complete this installation:

vCenter Server 6.0 U2
MS SQL Server 2014 (As of 7/10/16, this is the highest version supported for vCenter 6.0 U2)
SQL Server Native Client version 11 64 bit:
http://go.microsoft.com/fwlink/?LinkID=239648&clcid=0x409

Microsoft has released the Microsoft ODBC SQL Driver version 11 and the vCenter installer does not like it for the DSN you will create later. Make sure to stick with version 11 of the Native Client.
Windows Server 2012R2 (Upload this to a datastore for easy access)

I'm also making the assumption that you have an Active Directory domain already set up.

A quick overview of what we are going to do:

1. Deploy three Windows virtual machines.
PSC (Platform Services Controller)
SQL Server
vCenter Server
2. Configure a database inside of SQL for vCenter.
3. Configure the proper DSN on the vCenter Server.
4. Install the Platform Services Controller.
5. Install the vCenter Server.

Deploying Virtual Machines

1. Open and log into the vSphere Client for Windows.

INSERT SCREENSHOT for #2

2. Right click on your host and select New Virtual Machine.

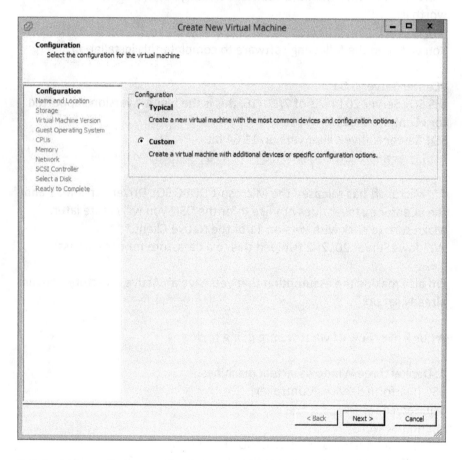

3. Select the radio button for Custom and click Next.

4. Enter the name for your virtual machine and click Next.

This should match the hostname of the server.

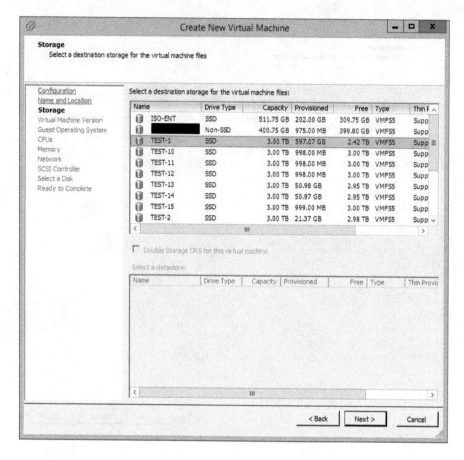

5. Choose the datastore where you will store the virtual machine and click Next.

6. Choose Virtual Machine Version 11 and click Next.

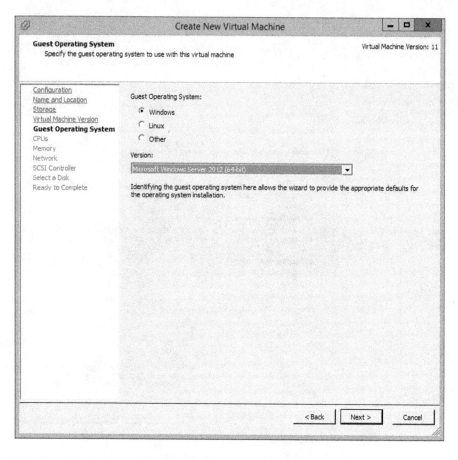

7. Select the radio button for Windows and use the drop down menu to select Windows 2012 (64-bit) and click Next.

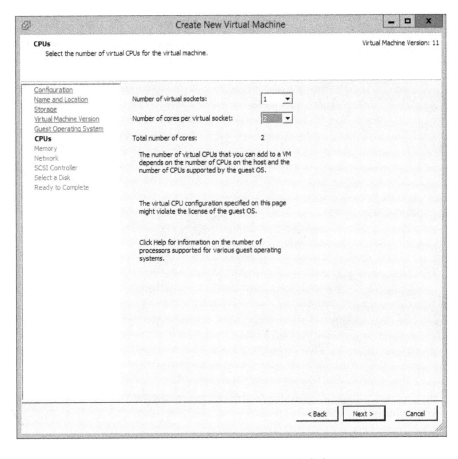

8. Use the drop down menu to select 2 cores and click Next.

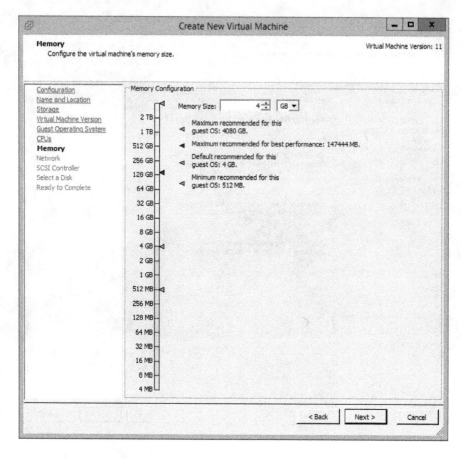

9. Take the default of 4GB and click Next. (For the specific vCenter virtual machine you will need 8GB or more.)

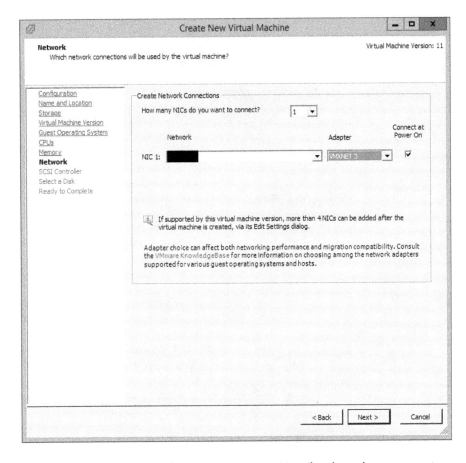

10. Select the VM Network you want to use. Use the drop down menu to select VMXNET3 and click Next.

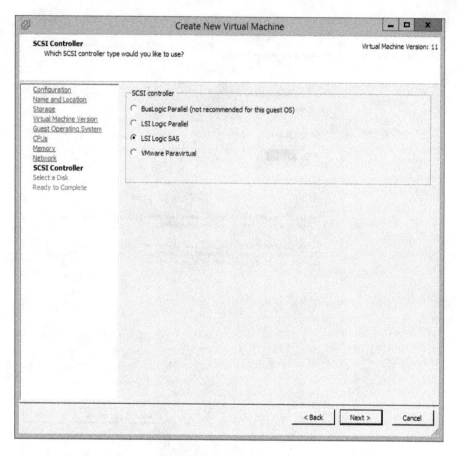

11. The SCSI controller is defaulted based on the Operating System profile you chose earlier. Leave the default and click Next.

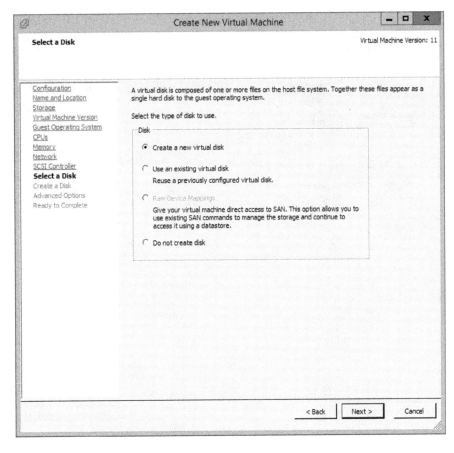

12. Select the radio button for Create a new virtual disk and click Next.

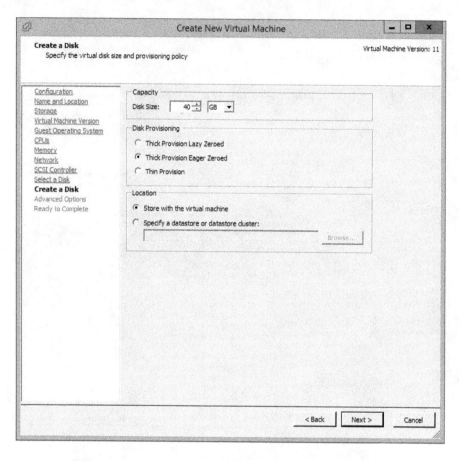

13. Leave the default disk size. Select the disk provisioning based on the best practices for the storage array you are using and click Next.

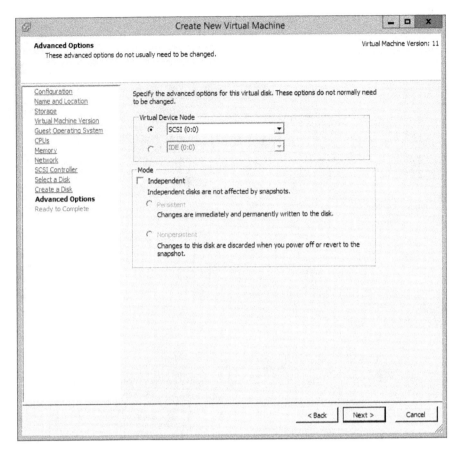

14. Leave the SCSI controller defaults and click Next.

Ready to Complete
Click Finish to start a task that will create the new virtual machine

Virtual Machine Version: 11

Configuration
Name and Location
Storage
Virtual Machine Version
Guest Operating System
CPUs
Memory
Network
SCSI Controller
Select a Disk
Create a Disk
Advanced Options
Ready to Complete

Settings for the new virtual machine:

Name:	PSC01
Host/Cluster:	TEST01.TEST.LAB
Datastore:	TEST-1
Guest OS:	Microsoft Windows Server 2012 (64-bit)
CPUs:	2
Memory:	4096 MB
NICs:	1
NIC 1 Network:	
NIC 1 Type:	VMXNET 3
SCSI Controller:	LSI Logic SAS
Create disk:	New virtual disk
Disk capacity:	40 GB
Disk provisioning:	Thick Provision Eager Zeroed
Datastore:	TEST-1
Virtual Device Node:	SCSI (0:0)
Disk mode:	Persistent

☑ Edit the virtual machine settings before completion

⚠ Creation of the virtual machine (VM) does not include automatic installation of the guest operating system. Install a guest OS on the VM after creating the VM.

< Back   Continue   Cancel

15. Review the information on this screen and check the box to edit the virtual machine configuration and click Continue.

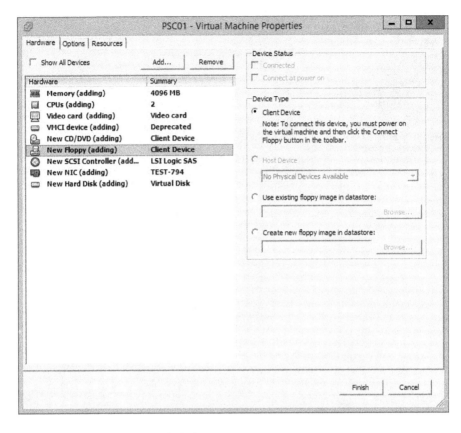

16. Select New Floppy and click Remove.

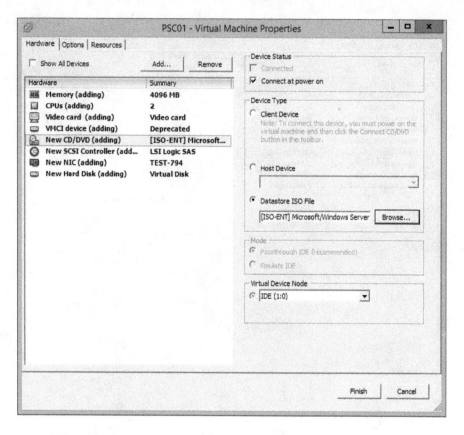

17. Select new CD/DVD and select the radio button for Datastore ISO file, check the box for Connect at Power on and click Browse.

18. Select the ISO you uploaded and click OK.

19. Click Finish.

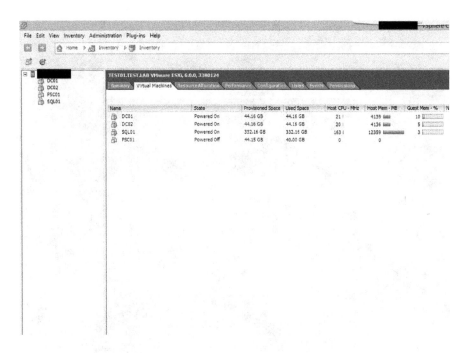

20. Right click on the new virtual machine and click Power > Power On.

21. Right click on the new virtual machine and click Open Console.

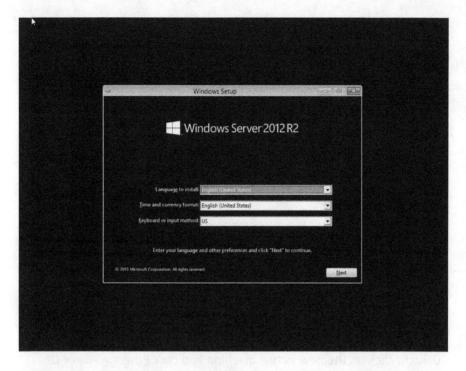

22. Leave the defaults and click Next.

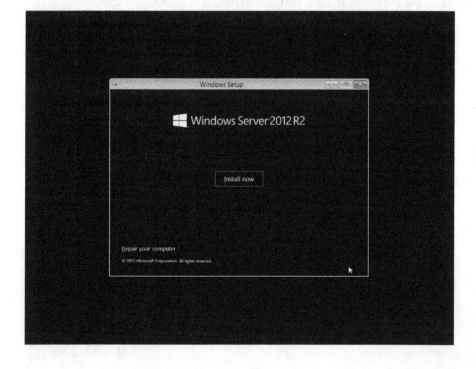

23. Click Install Now.

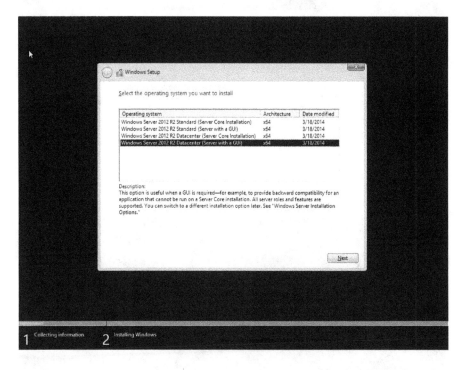

24. Select the appropriate Windows server version and click Next. (It must have the GUI.)

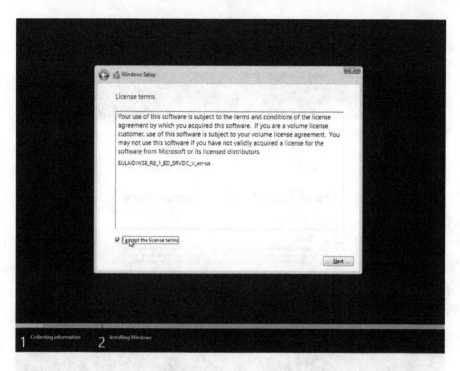

25. Check the box for I accept and click Next.

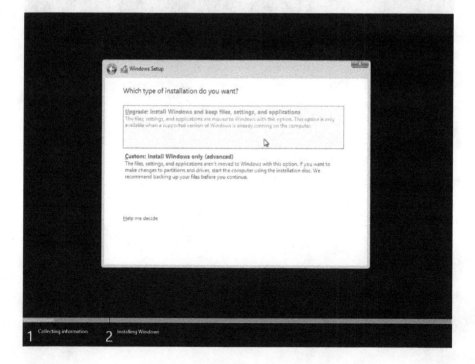

26. Click Custom: Install Windows only (advanced).

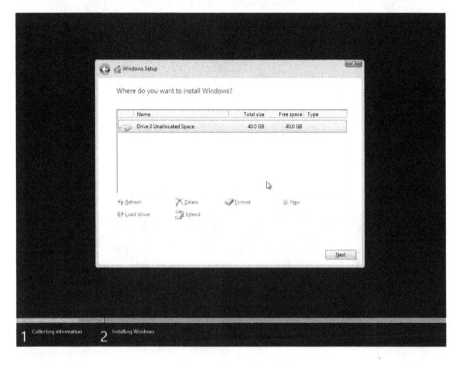

27. Select the disk and click New.

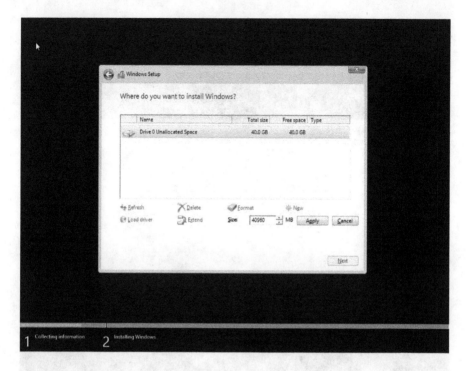

28. Click Apply.

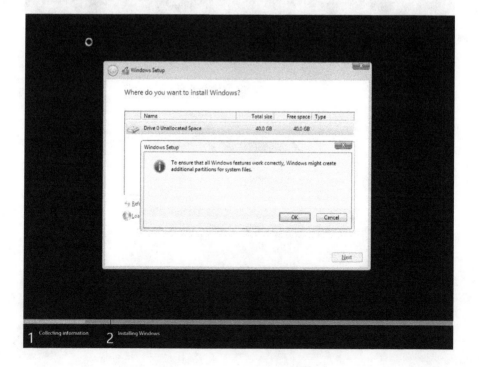

29. Click OK.

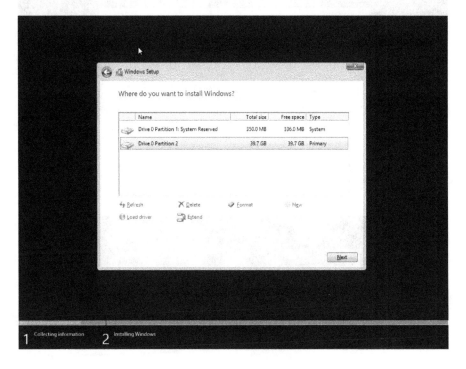

30. Make sure it created two partitions and select the Primary and click Next.

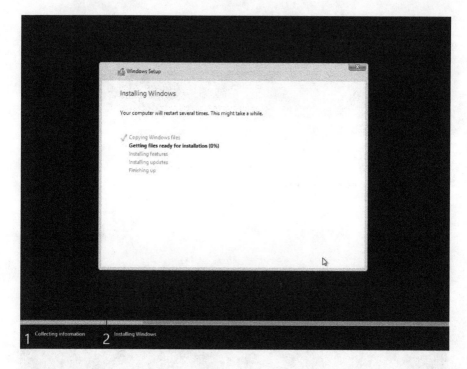

31. The system will begin to install then it will automatically reboot when it has completed.

Settings

Type a password for the built-in administrator account that you can use to sign in to this computer.

User name   Administrator

Password

Reenter password

Finish

32. Enter a password for the Administrator account and click Finish.

Press Ctrl+Alt+Delete to sign in.

3:38
Sunday, July 10

33. Right click on the virtual machine and click Guest > Send Control-Alt-Delete.

34. Enter the password for the administrator account and hit Enter.

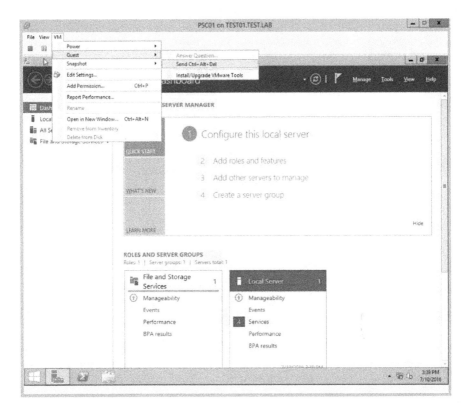

35. After the login has completed, choose VM > Guest > Install/Upgrade VMWare Tools.

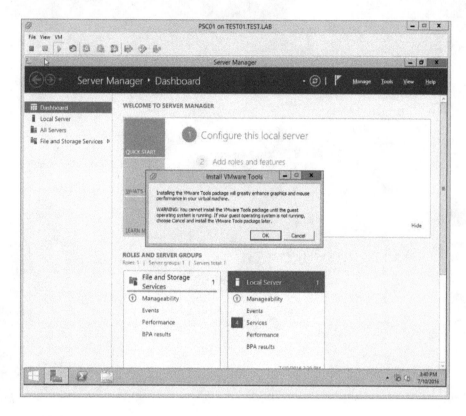

36. Click OK.

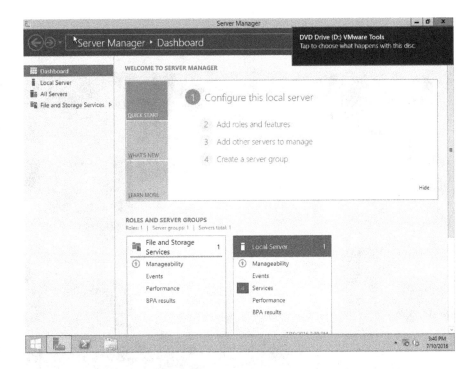

37. Click the Blue Banner and Click Run.

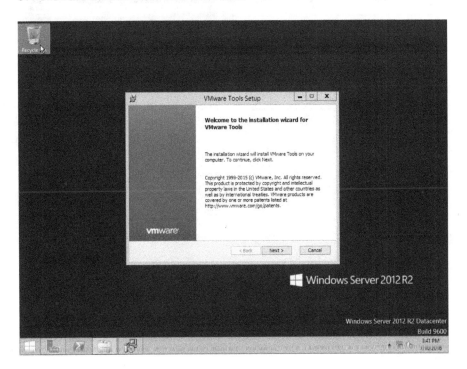

38. Click Next.

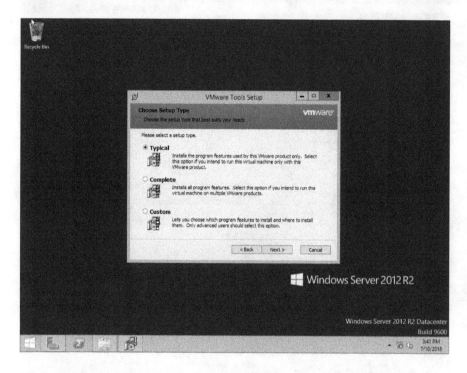

39. Select the radio button for Typical and click Next.

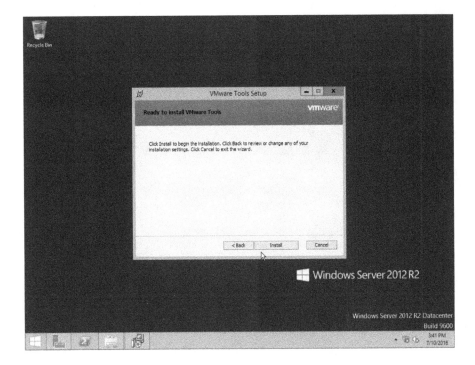

40. Click Install.

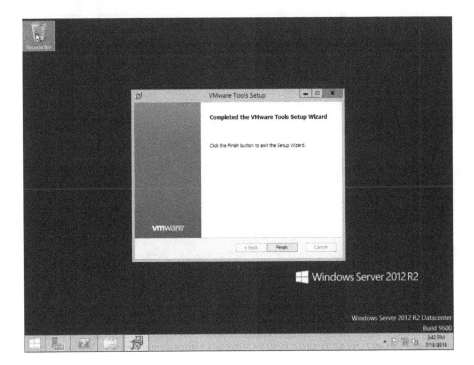

41. After the install is complete, click Finish.

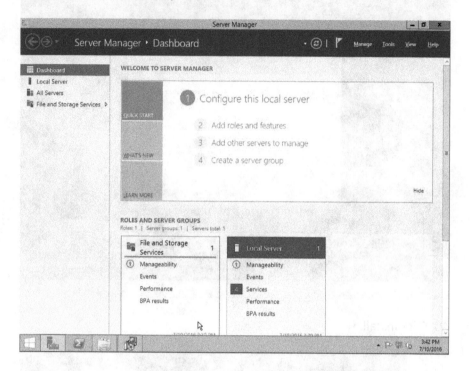

42. Click the Briefcase and Refrigerator looking icon in the lower left.

43. Click Local Server.

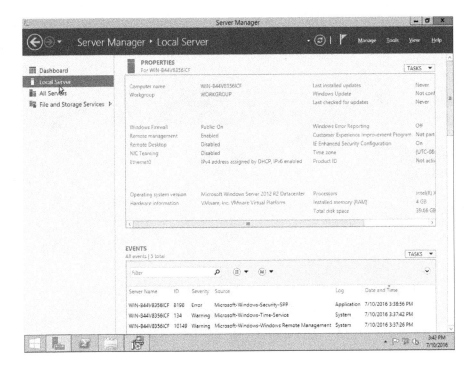

44. Click Disabled next to Remote Desktop.

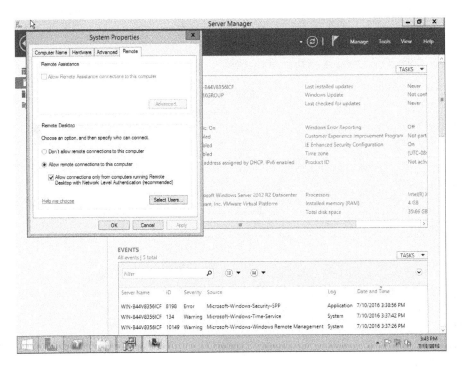

45. Select the radio button next to allow remote connections, click OK, click OK again.

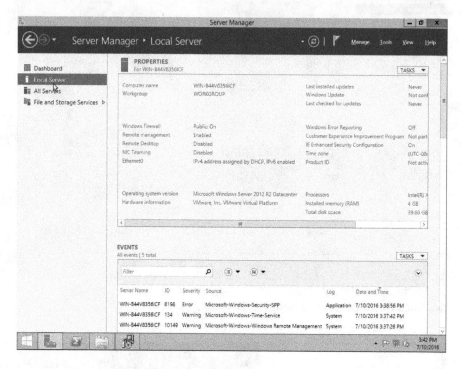

46. Click IPv4 address assigned by DHCP.

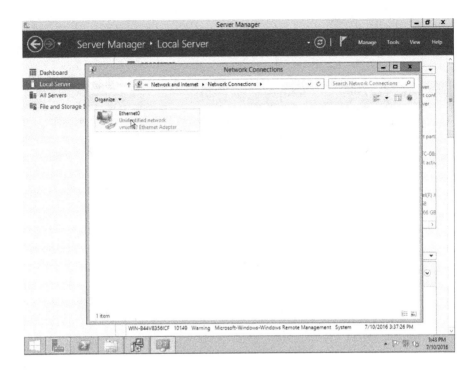

47. Double click on Ethernet0.

48. Click Properties.

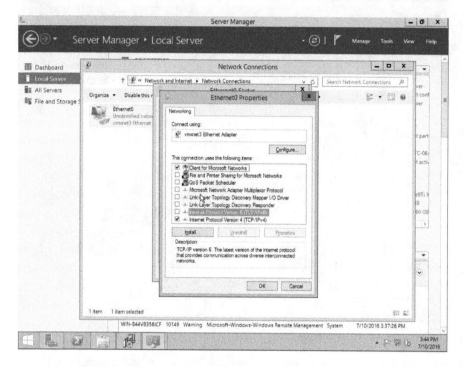

49. The only things that should be checked are:
   Client for Microsoft Networks
   File and Printer Sharing for Microsoft Networks
   Internet Protocol Version 4 (TCP/IPv4)

50. Double click on Internet Protocol Version 4 (TCP/IPv4).

51. Enter the IP address, Net mask, Gateway, and DNS servers.

52. Click OK. Click OK.

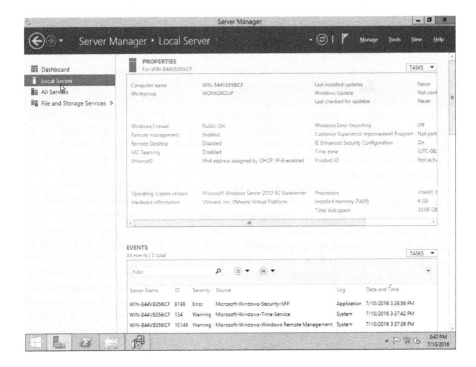

53. Click ON next to IE Enhanced Security Configuration.

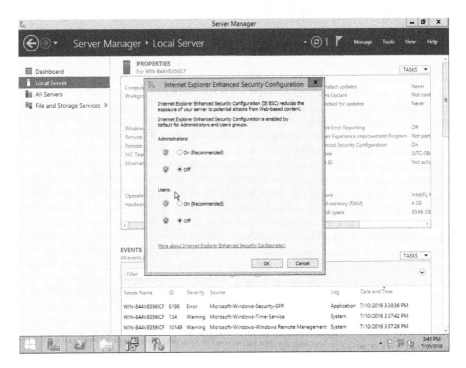

54. Select the radio buttons for Off in both sections. Click OK.

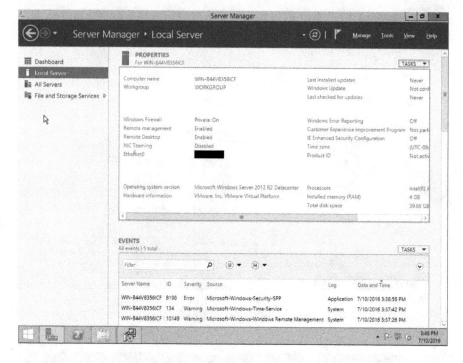

55. Click the random name next to Computer Name.

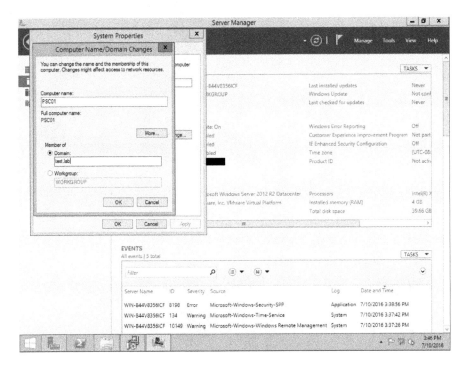

56. Click Change. Enter the name for the virtual machine.

57. Select the radio button for Domain and enter the domain name and click OK.

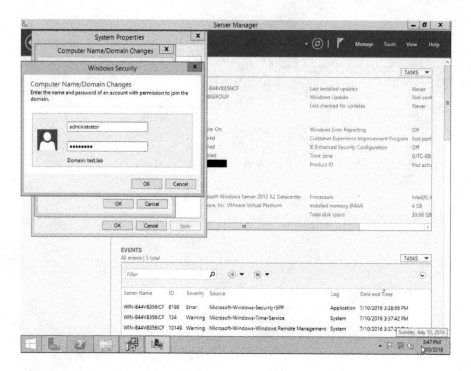

58. Enter the domain administrator credentials or an account who has permissions to add computers to the domain and click OK.

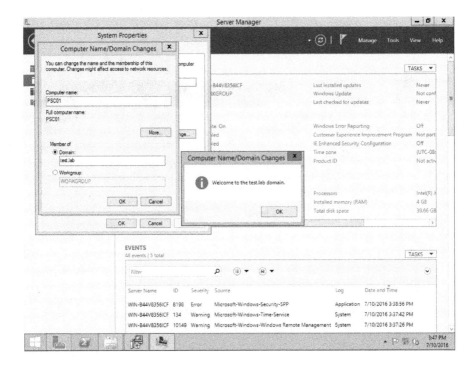

59. You should receive the success message. Click OK.

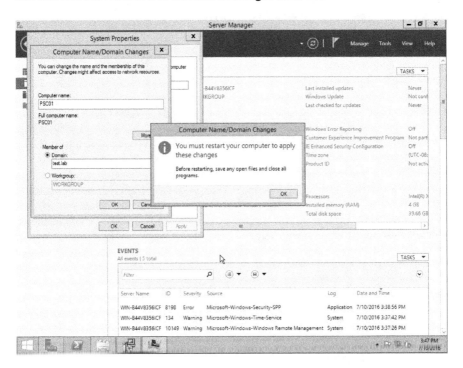

60. Click OK.

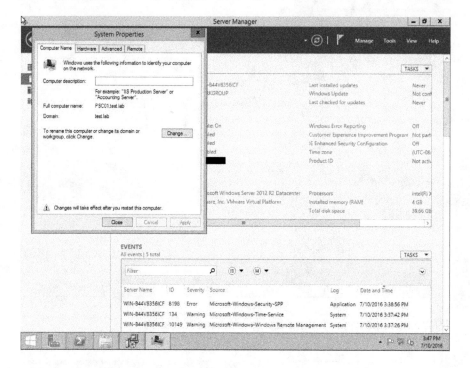

61. Click Close.

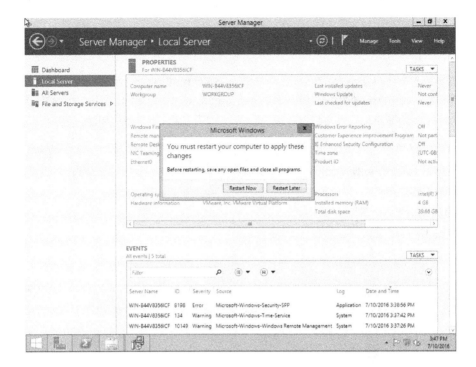

62. Click Restart Now.

Now your first virtual machine is created!

Repeat these steps for two more virtual machines. Select one machine for SQL Server and perform the necessary steps to install and configure SQL Server. That is out of scope of this document, but there will be another book about it.

You should now have three virtual machines:
Platform Services Controller (ours is PSC01)
vCenter Server (ours is VC01)
SQL Server (ours is SQL01)

Deploying vCenter External Platform Services Controller

1. Open the console and log into the Windows virtual machine you created for the platform services controller.

2. Copy the vCenter Server 6.0 U2 media to the desktop.

3. Right click on the ISO and click Mount.

4. Double click autorun.exe

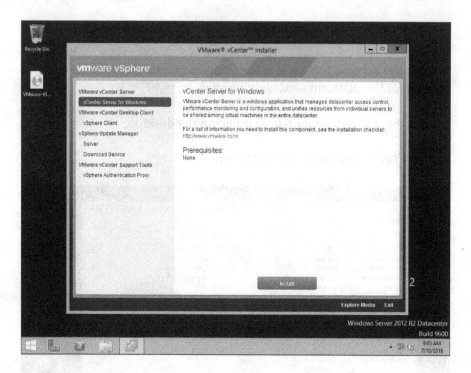

5. Select vCenter Server for Windows and click Install.

It may take a little bit to open the installer. Be patient.

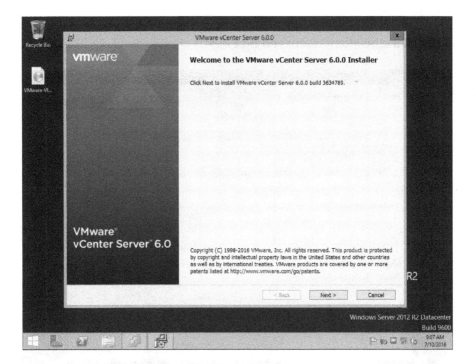

6. Once the install has finished loading, click Next.

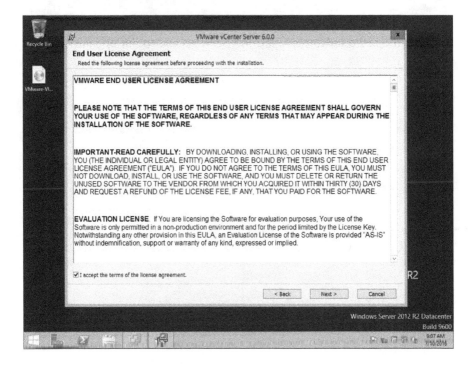

7. Check the box for I Accept and click Next.

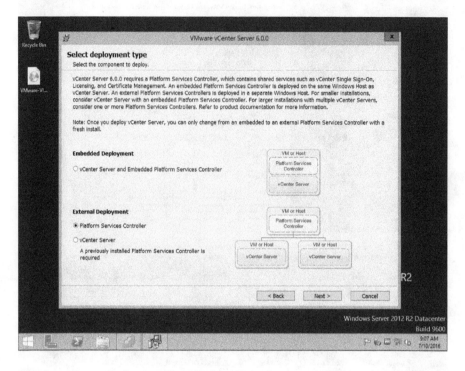

8. Select the radio button for Platform Services Controller and click Next.

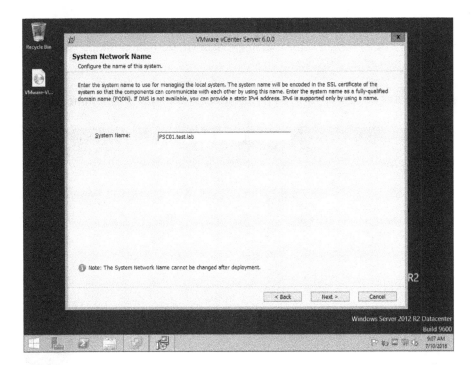

9. Make sure the FQDN is proper for this machine and click Next.

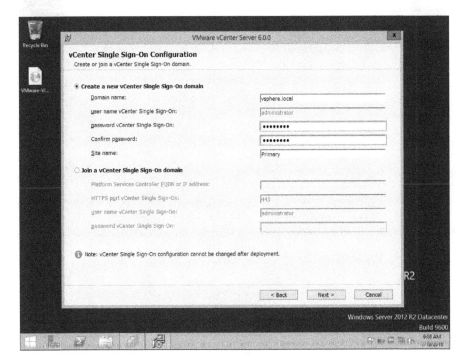

10. Enter a domain name for the Single-Sign On domain name, password and site name then click Next.

This cannot be the same as your Active Directory domain name.

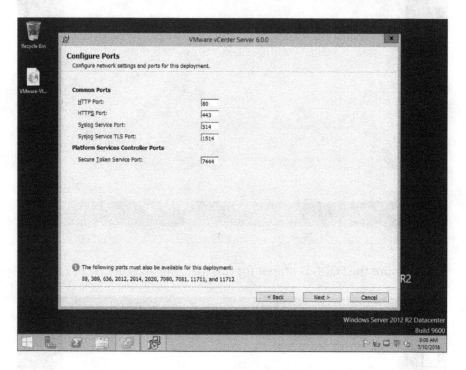

11. Take the defaults on this screen and click Next.

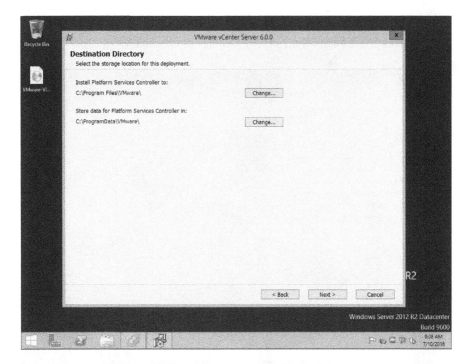

12. Take the defaults on this screen and click Next.

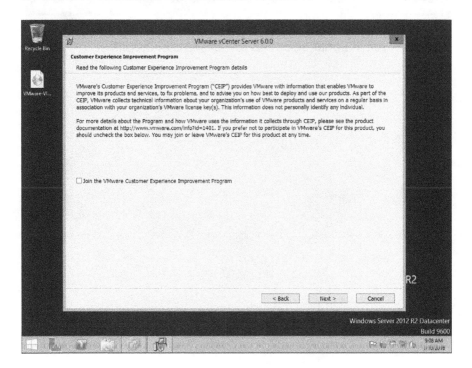

13. Uncheck the box for the Join the VMware and click Next.

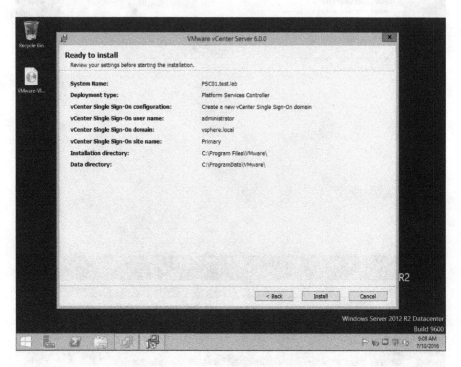

14. Review the information on this screen and click Install.

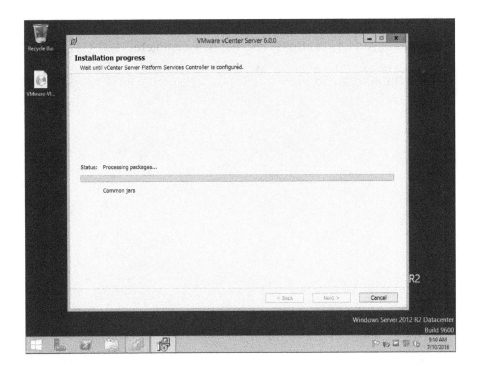

You will see the install begin and monitor it in case of any errors.

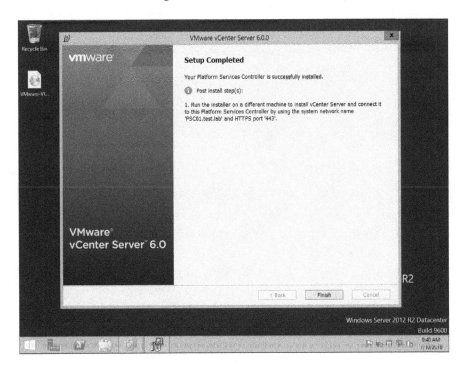

The platform services controller install is now complete!

15. Click Finish.

Configure SQL Server for vCenter Server for Windows

1. Log onto the virtual machine you have installed SQL Server on.

2. Open the SQL Server Management Studio.

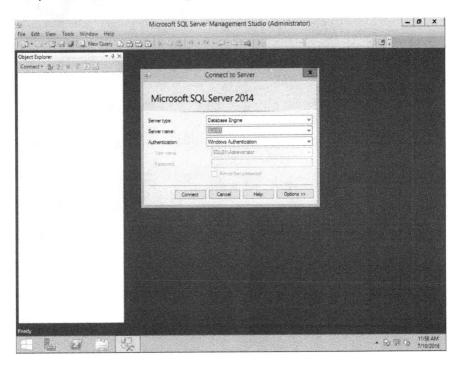

3. Enter your credentials and click Connect.

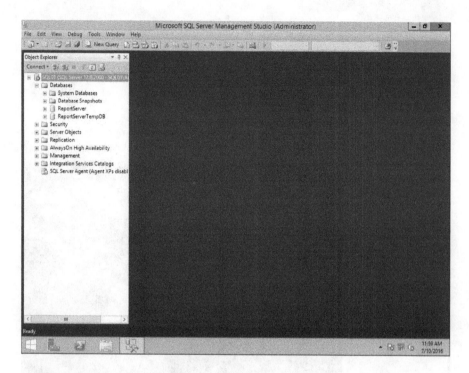

4. Click the + on Databases to Expand it. Right click on Databases and click
New Database.

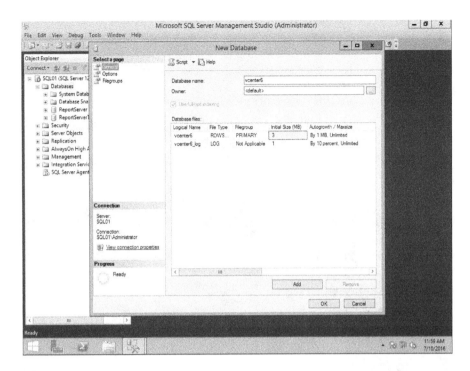

5. Type a name for the database and click OK.

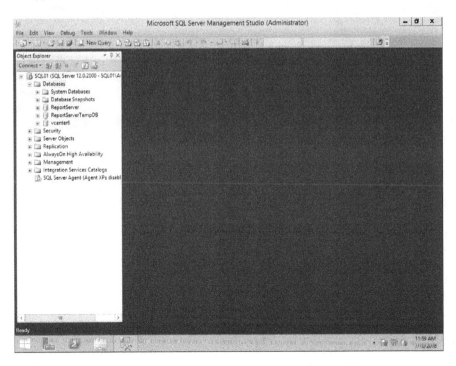

6. Verify that the database has been created.

7. Log off of the SQL Server.

8. Log onto the virtual machine you have designated for vCenter.

9. Copy the SQL Server 2012 Native Client to the desktop and double click it to run.

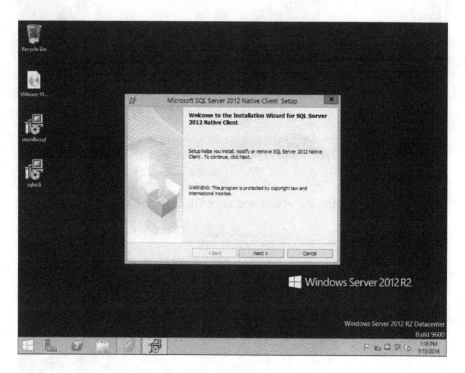

10. Click Next.

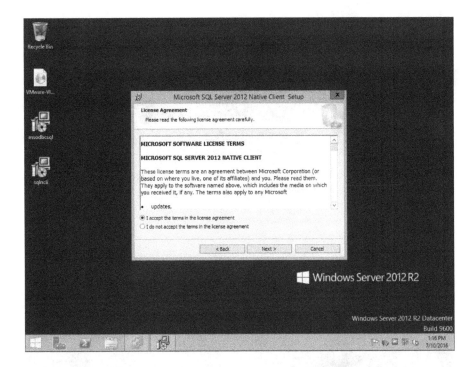

11. Select the radio button next to I Accept and click Next.

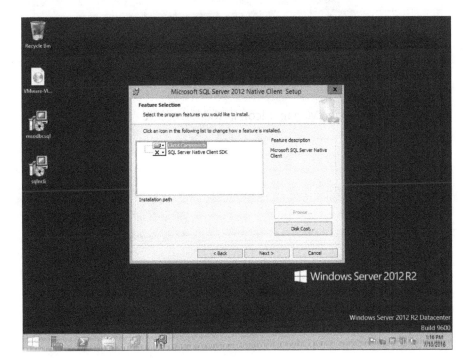

12. Click Next.

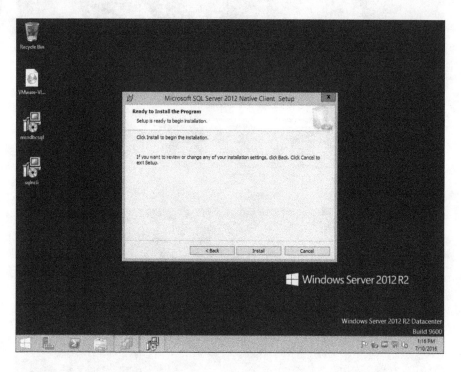

13. Click Install.

14. After the install has completed, Click Finish.

15. Click on the Server Manager icon in the lower left.

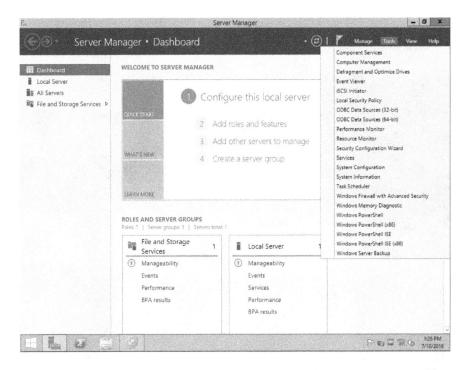

16. Click Tools and click ODBC Data Sources (64-bit).

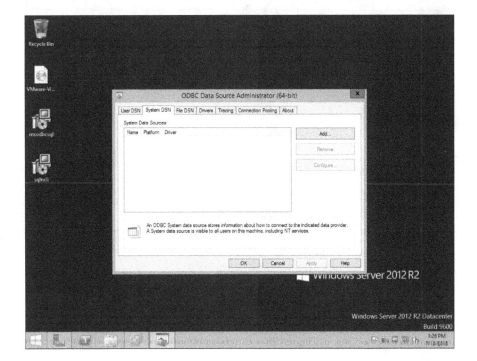

17. Click System DSN.

18. Click Add.

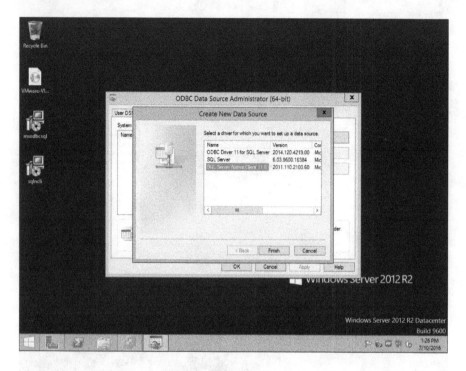

19. Select SQL Server Native Client 11.0 and click Finish.

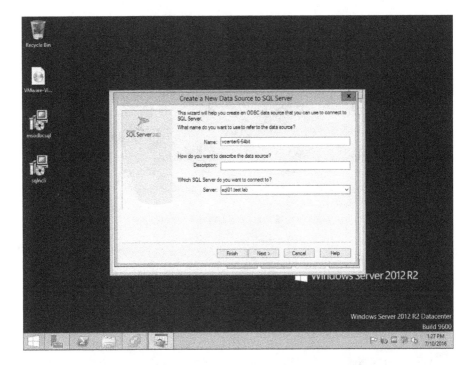

20. Enter a name for the DSN and the SQL Server. Click Next.

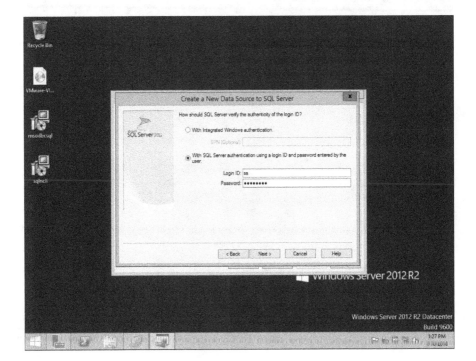

21. Select the radio button for Use SQL Server authentication, enter the username and password that has access and click Next.

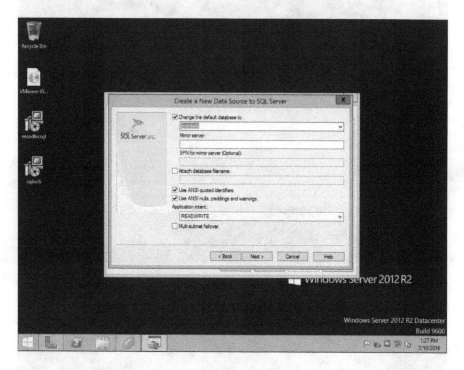

22. Check the box for Change the default database and use the drop down menu to select the database.

23. Click Next.

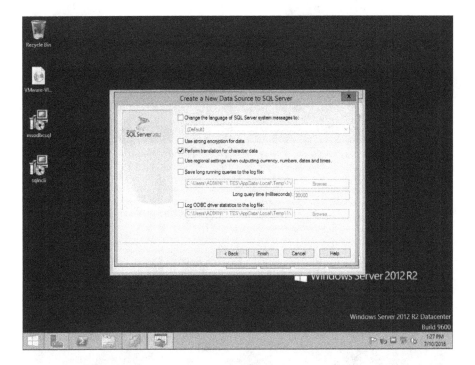

24. Leave the defaults and click Next.

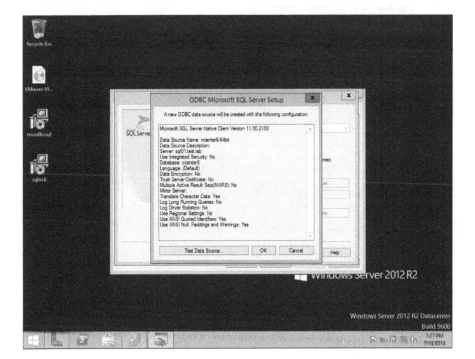

25. Click Test Data Source.

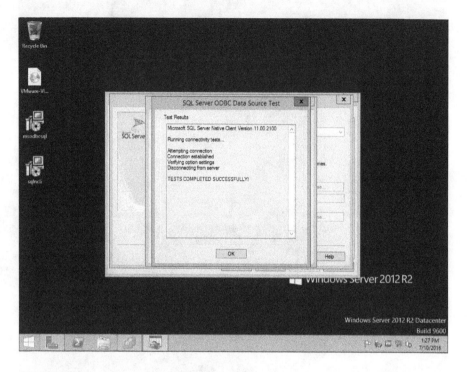

26. Click OK.

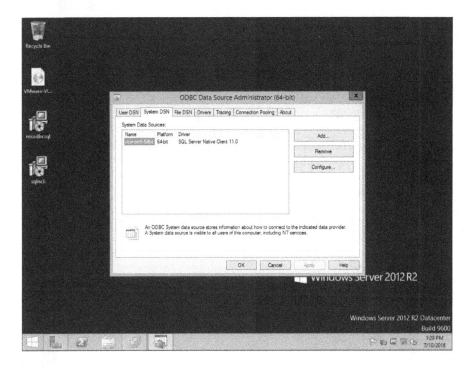

27. Click OK.

Deploy vCenter for Windows

1. Copy the media to the desktop and right click the ISO and click Mount.

2. Double click autorun.exe.

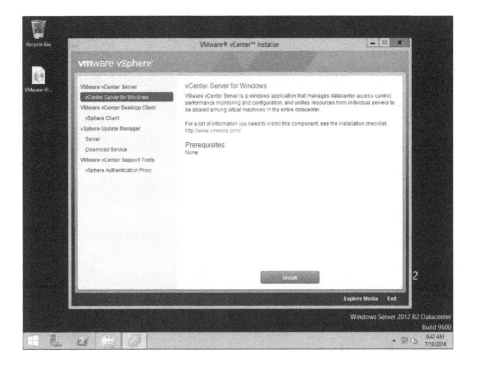

3. Select vCenter Server for Windows and click Install.

It may take a little bit to open the installer. Be patient.

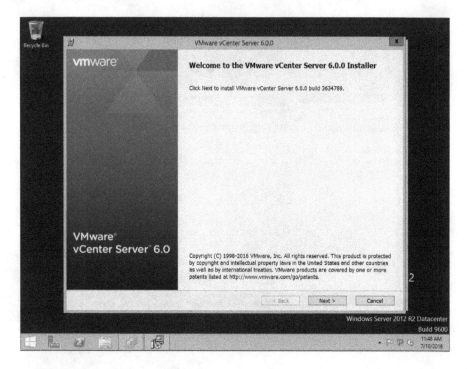

4. After the installer has finished loading, click Next.

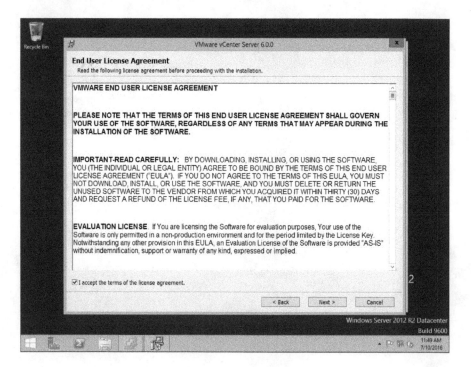

5. Check the box for I Accept and click Next.

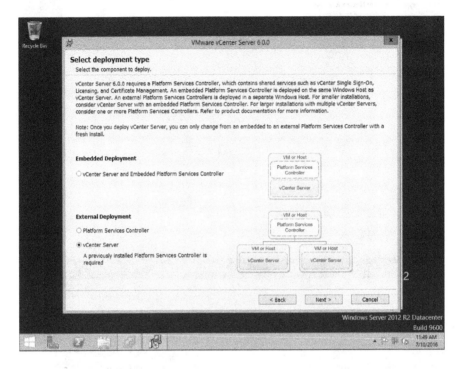

6. Select the radio button for vCenter Server and click Next.

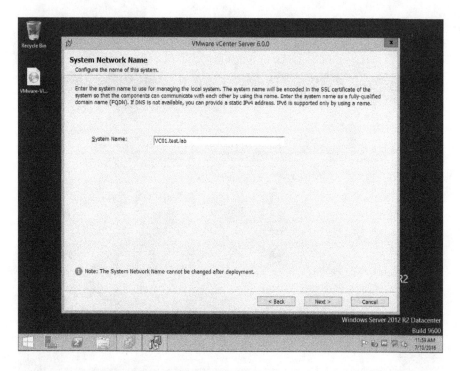

7. Verify the FQDN is correct and click Next.

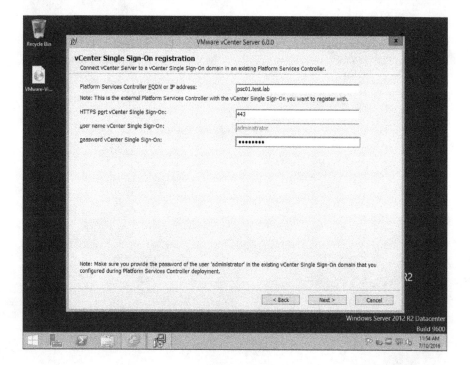

8. Enter the FQDN for the PSC and the password for the Single-Sign On administrator and click Next.

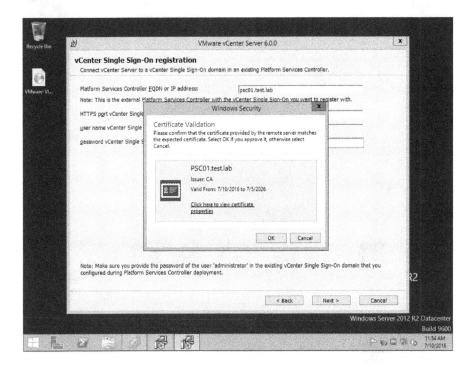

9. Click OK.

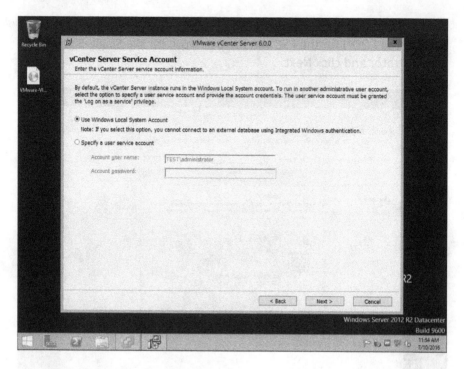

10. Leave the defaults and click Next.

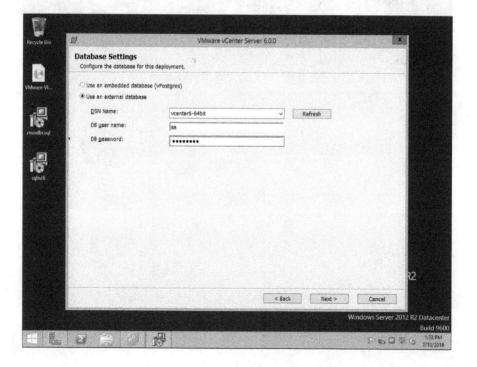

11. Select the radio button for Use an external database. Use the drop down menu to select the DSN you created.

12. Enter the username and password that has access to the database and click Next.

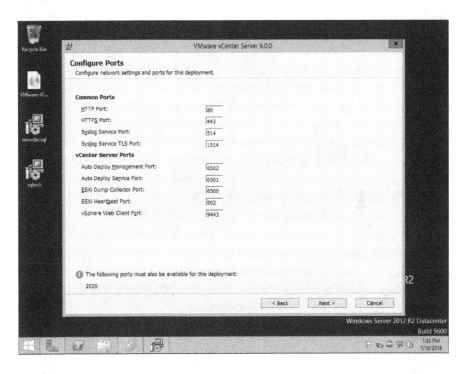

13. Leave the defaults here and click Next.

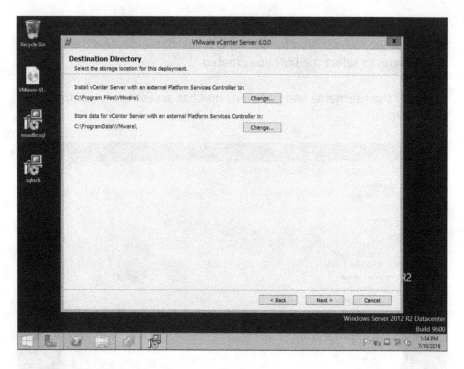

14. Leave the defaults here and click Next.

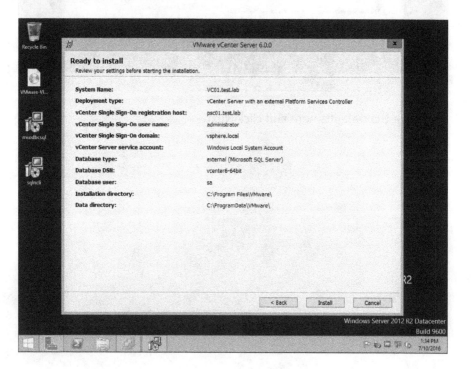

15. Click Install.

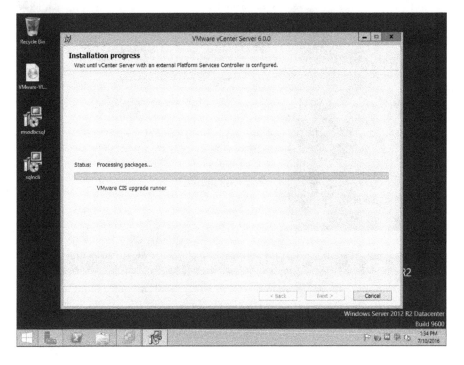

The installer will begin so you should monitor for any errors.

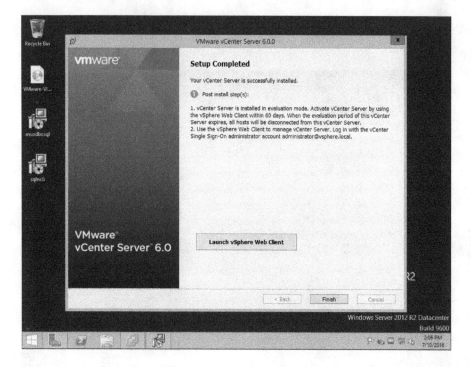

The install has been completed!

16. Click Finish.

The next step is to configure the vCenter Server!

Deploy vCenter Server Appliance

In this section, we are going to deploy the vCenter Server Appliance.

If you are going into a production environment, you should not do an embedded PSC. vCenter always seems to run better in a separated scenario. Just my experience at least.

There are going to be some pre-requisites that you need to accomplish:

1. Install the vSphere Client Integration Plugin.
2. Enter the DNS name and IP address into DNS prior to install.
3. Verify NTP server.
4. Your SSO domain should not match your Active Directory or other LDAP domain.

A couple notes to be aware of because I had some serious issues deploying this:

1. You may need to deploy from a server that is in the subnet you are deploying to.
2. You may need to create entries in your local host file that mirror the DNS entries.
3. Do not enter more than one DNS server.
4. Do not use a NTP server yet. Synchronize with the host first and configure the NTP after.
5. You should deploy to a host that is currently using a Standard Switch. A Distributed Switch seems to block the install.

Deploy an External Platform Services Controller

Once you have your media, go ahead and mount it with the appropriate tool that you use.

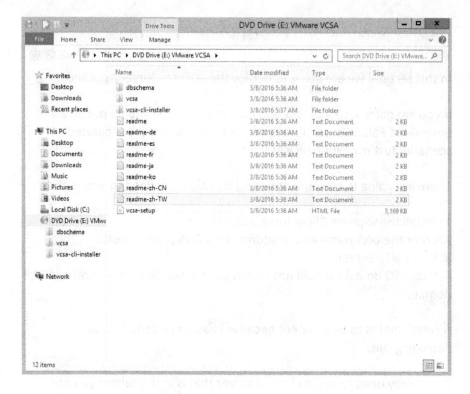

1. Double click on the vcsa-setup.html file.

1. Please install the Client Integration Plugin 6.0 provided in the vCenter Server Appliance ISO image (requires quitting the browser).
2. When prompted, allow access to the Client Integration Plugin.
   Detecting Client Integration Plugin... 27sec

The browser will start to detect the Client Integration Plugin.

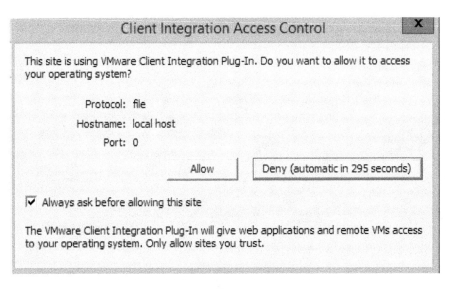

2. Click Allow to access the Client Integration Plugin.

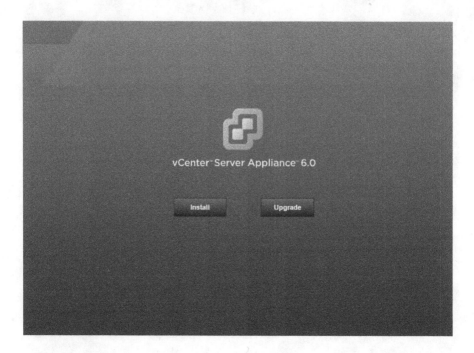

3. Click Install.

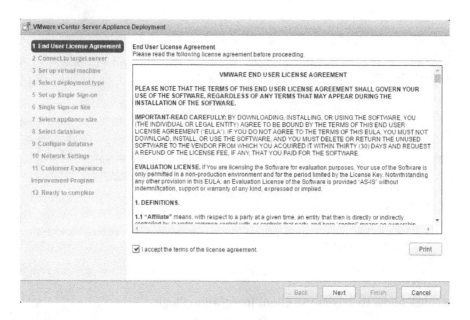

4. Check the box for I accept and click Next.

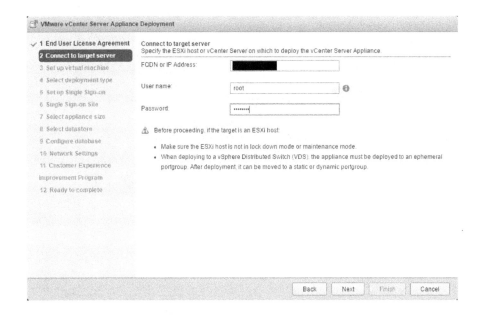

5. Enter the IP address of your host, root credentials and click Next.

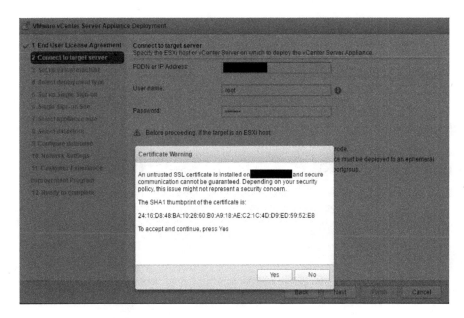

6. Click Yes to accept the self-signed certificate.

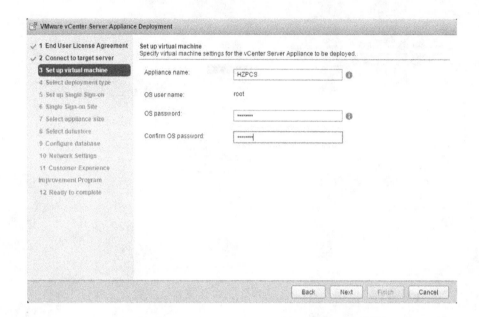

7. Enter a name for the appliance, a root password and click Next.

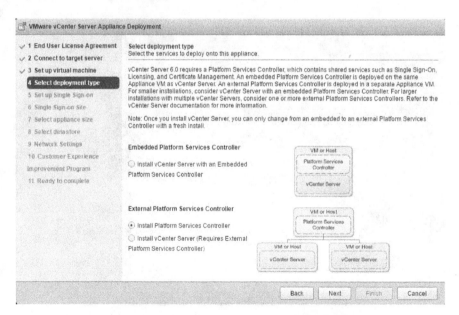

8. Select the radio button for Install Platform Services Controller.

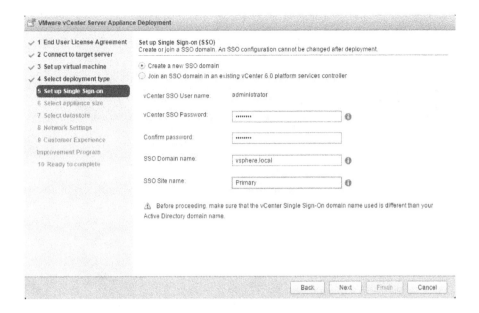

9. Select the radio button for Create a new SSO domain.

10. Enter a password, domain name, and site name.

DO NOT USE YOUR ACTIVE DIRECTORY DOMAIN NAME. (Sorry for the all caps. Its important.)

11. Click Next.

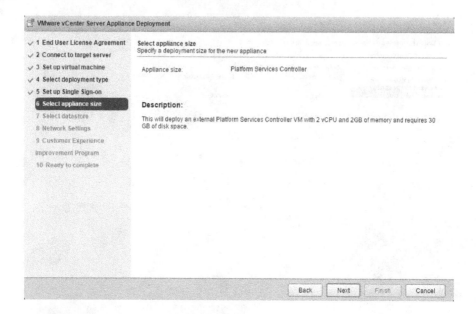

12. Click Next.

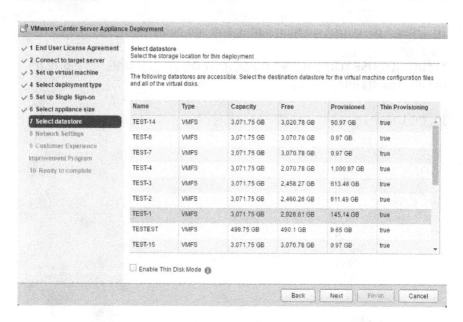

13. Select a datastore and click Next.

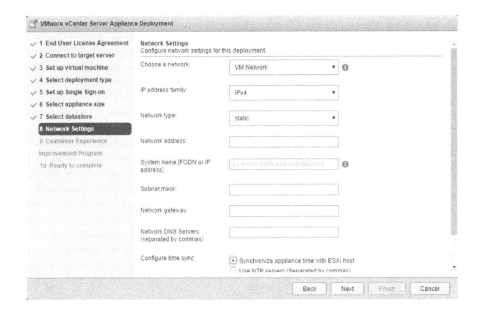

14. Enter the IP address information, the FQDN and don't forget to select Synchronize with Host and click Next.

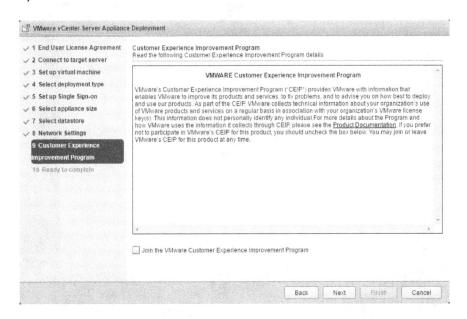

15. Uncheck the box for Join and click Next.

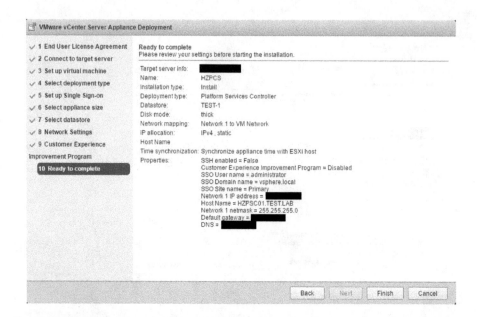

16. Review the information and click Finish.

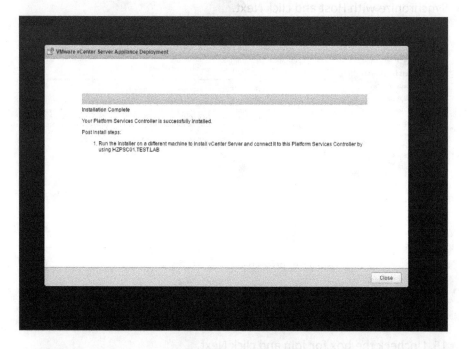

Eventually your installation will complete and you will get this message. If it fails for whatever reason, go back to the beginning of this section and make sure you have followed my advice.

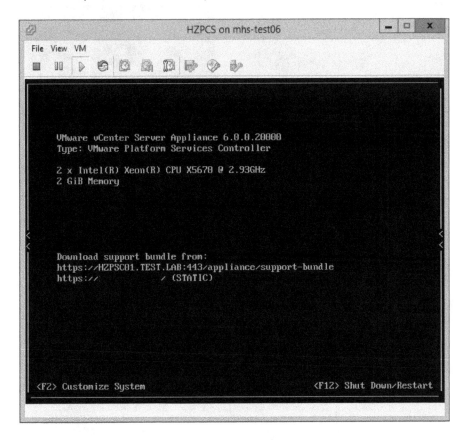

You can verify it is up and running by opening the console of the virtual machine.

17. Click Close to return to the main screen.

Deploy a vCenter Server Appliance

1. Click Install.

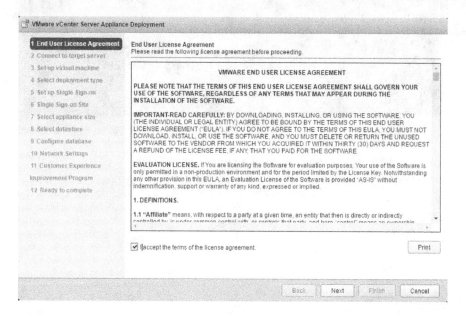

2. Check the box for I accept and click Next.

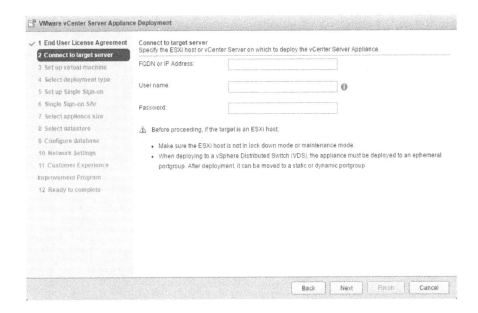

3. Enter the IP address of your host, root credentials and click Next.

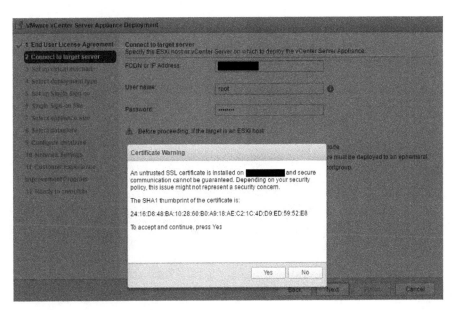

4. Click Yes to accept the self-signed certificate.

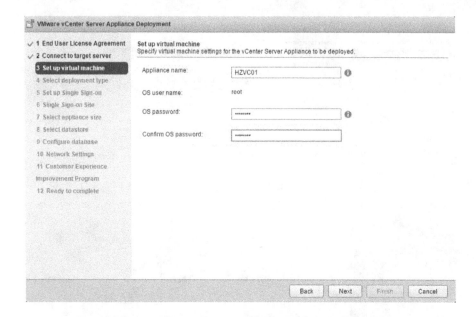

5. Enter a name for the appliance, a root password and click Next.

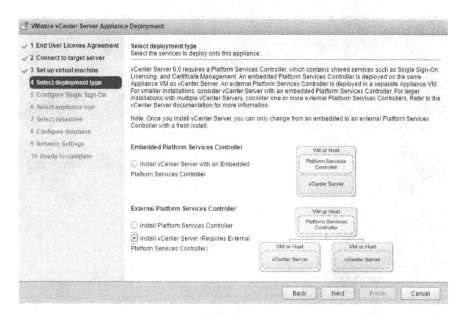

6. Select the radio button for Install vCenter Server and click Next.

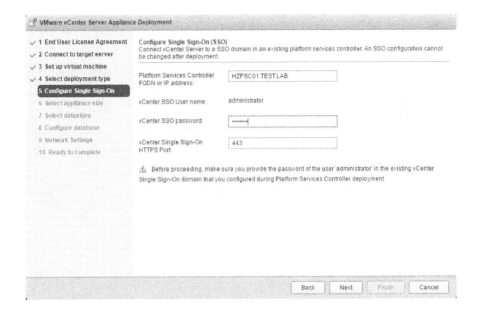

7. Enter the information for the External PSC and click Next.

8. Select the size that corresponds to the environment you are setting up and click Next.

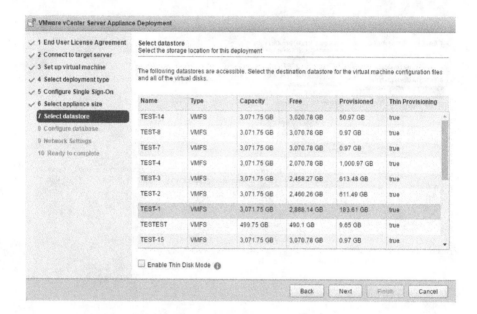

9. Select a datastore and click Next.

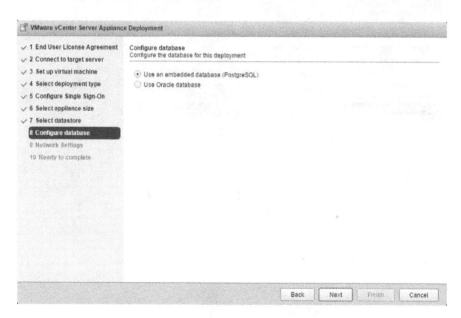

10. Select the radio button for Use an embedded database.

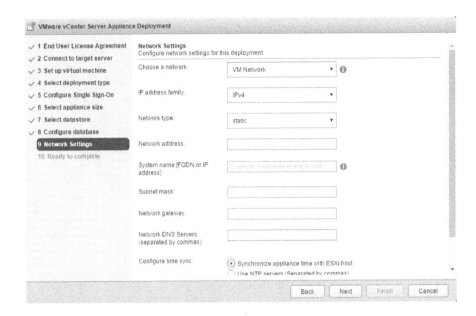

11. Enter the IP address information, the FQDN and don't forget to select Synchronize with Host and click Next.

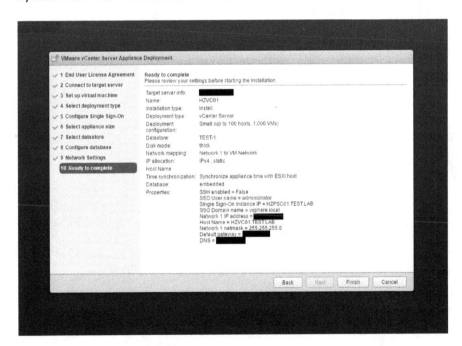

12. Review the information and click Finish.

Installation Complete

Your vCenter Server is successfully installed.

Post install steps:

1. vCenter Server is installed in evaluation mode. Activate vCenter Server by using the vSphere Web Client within 60 days. When the evaluation period of this vCenter Server expires, all hosts will be disconnected from this vCenter Server.
2. Use the vSphere Web Client to manage vCenter Server. Log in with the Single Sign-On administrator account administrator@vsphere.local

You can now login to vSphere Web Client: https://HZVC01.TESTLAB/vsphere-client as administrator@vsphere.local

Close

After this installation completes, you will receive this message with the URL for your new vCenter! Woo!

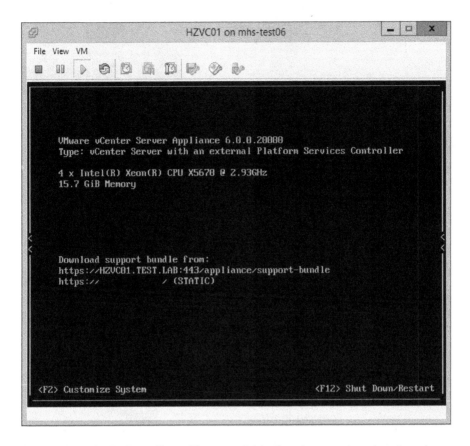

You can verify the install just like you did before by opening the virtual machine console.

Configure the External PSC and vCenter Server Appliances

Now before you check out your new vCenter, let's do a little configuration.

1. Open a browser to the following locations:

https://fqdnofpsc:5480/
https://fqdnofvc:5480/

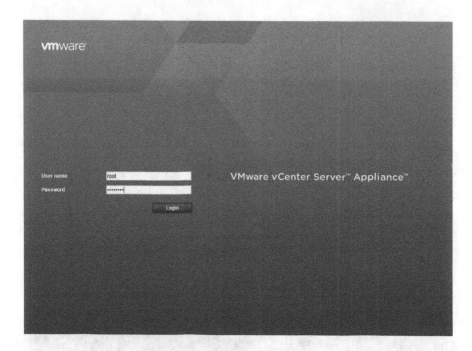

If you aren't new to vSphere, you will notice something different than the old appliances. They updated the interface!

2. Log in with your root credentials.

3. Review the summary tab and click Access.

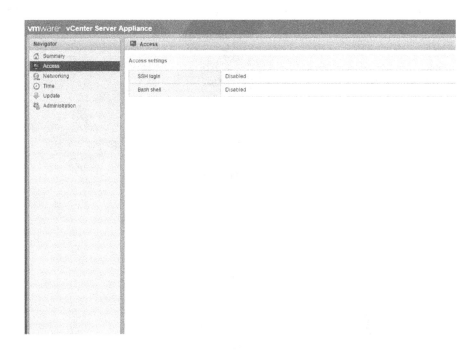

4. This is where you can enable the shell access. Click Networking.

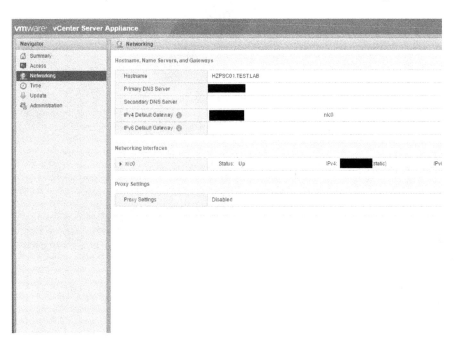

5. Here you can review your IP info and set another DNS server. Click

Time.

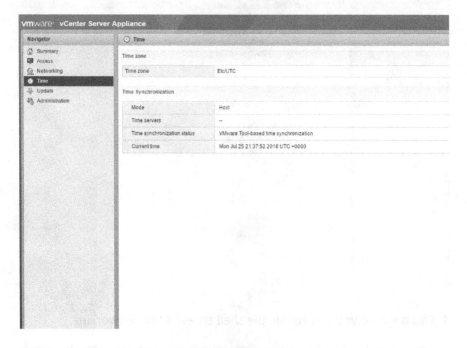

6. Here you can set your Time Zone and add NTP servers. Click Update.

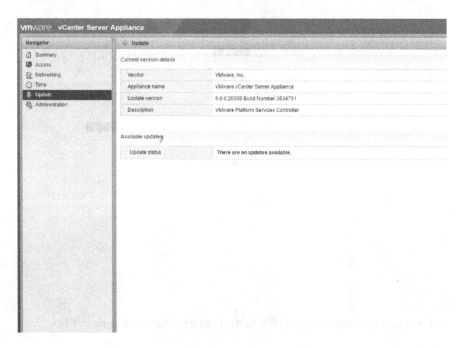

7. Here you can see the appliance information note it says Platform Services Controller.

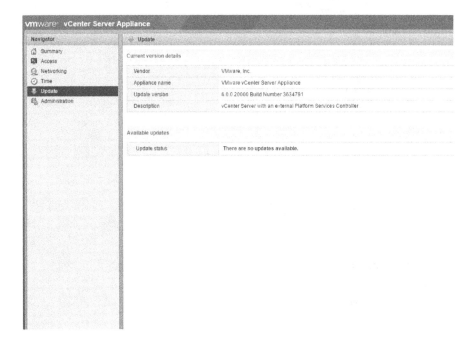

8. Here is what the vCenter Server appliance information looks like. Click Administration.

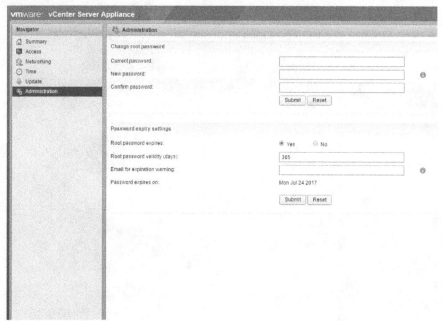

9. Here you can change the root password and all that jazz.

We are done! Now onto configuring vCenter!

Configure vCenter

From here on out, we will be using the vCenter Web Client to configure everything that is possible for that. I personally love the thick client but VMware has decided to deprecate it and not add any new functions. Oh well. You must assimilate at some point. Might as well do it now.

This is going to be basic configuration for vCenter just to get some stuff up and running smoothly. Here are the areas we will be covering:

Administration
Host and Clusters
Storage
Networking
Availability
Host Management
Virtual Machine Management

This will get us a fully functioning vCenter ready for fun activities to come.

Configuring vCenter Administration

1. Open a web browser of your choice and navigate to the DNS name or IP that you configured for the vCenter virtual machine.

You may get some messages about SSL errors. No worries just continue on through them and you will get to the next screen

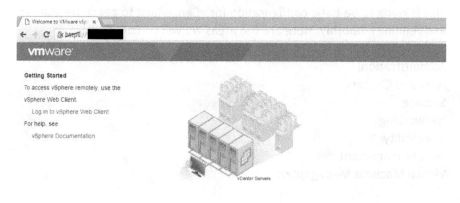

2. Click Log in to vSphere Web Client.

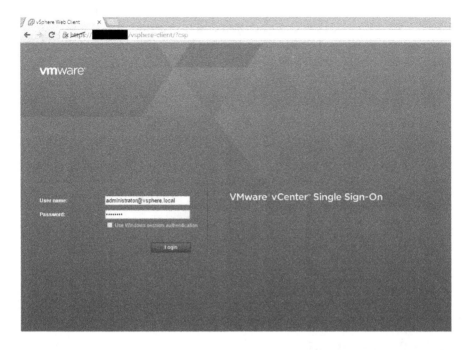

3. You will receive a pop up box saying to allow the vSphere Client Integration Plugin. This is required so click Allow.

4. Enter the administrator with the SSO domain that you created and its password and click Login.

EX: administrator@vsphere.local is what I used.

Now you have arrived at the vSphere Web Client homepage. This where you will start for all of the configuration and management tasks. We see a warning at the top saying that your vCenter has expiring licenses. This is because you are in evaluation mode.

5. Click Manage Licenses in the warning bar.

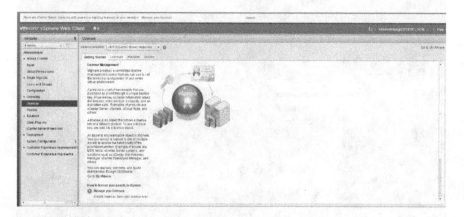

6. Click the Licenses tab in the right pane.

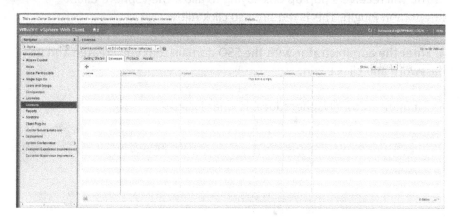

As you can see the licenses are empty.

7. Click the green +.

8. Enter your License keys from the VMware portal each on its on line.

9. Click Next when you are ready.

10. Create an easily identifiable label for each continue and click Next.

11. Click Finish.

You should see your keys in this window now.

12. Click the Assets tab in the right pane to continue.

13. Right click on your vCenter and click Assign license.

14. Select the radio button next to the vCenter license and click OK.

You can see that your vCenter is now licensed.

15. Click the X at the far right of the warning bar to close the message.

16. Click Configuration under Single Sign On in the left pane to continue.

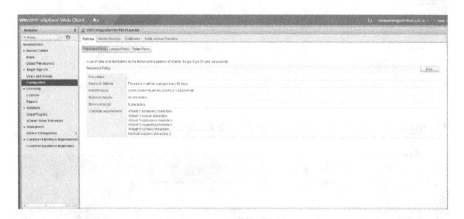

This is the password policies for local users configured in vCenter.

17. Click Edit to configure.

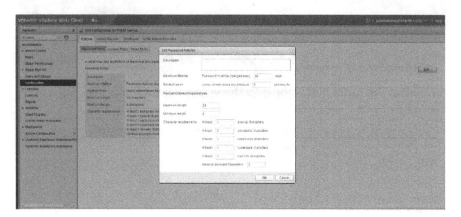

18. Set the password policies that you would like and click OK.

19. Click the Lockout Policy tab.

20. Click Edit.

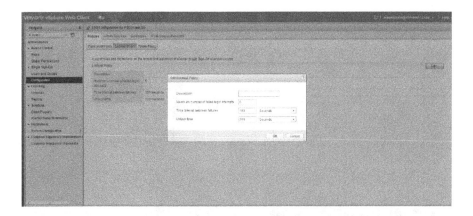

21. Set the lockout policies that you would like and click OK.

22. Click Users and Groups under Single Sign On.

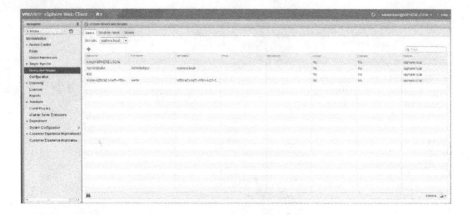

Here is where you will create local users for vCenter.

23. Click the green +.

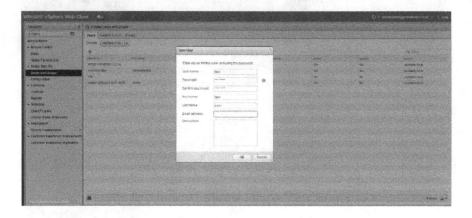

24. Fill out the box and click OK.

25. Now that your user appears, click Groups.

26. Scroll down and highlight the Administrators group. Click the + with a person next to it in the lower pane.

27. Select the user you created by double clicking and click OK.

28. Click Configuration under Single Sign On and then click Identity Sources.

29. Click the green +.

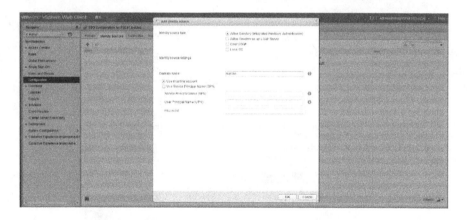

Since this is a Windows machine you can use the computer account to read the domain information.

30. Select the radio button next to Active Directory (Integrated Windows Authentication) and click OK.

Now your identity source appears in the list.

31. Click Users and Groups and then Groups.

32. Click the People+.

33. In the Domain drop down, choose your Active Directory domain and double click a group to add it to the list. Click OK.

34. Click Roles under Access Control.

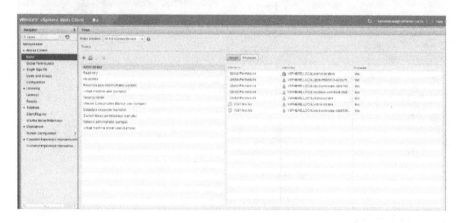

This is the list of roles available on vCenter by default. You can create your own custom roles to meet the needs of your organization.

35. Click Global Permissions.

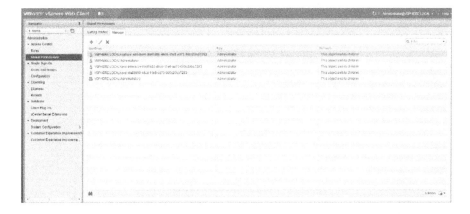

36. Click the Manage tab and then click the green +.

37. Select Administrator under the Assigned Role and click Add.

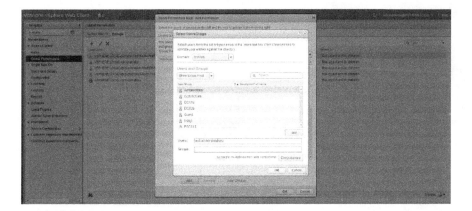

38. Select your Active Directory domain from the drop down list and double click your Domain Administrator or another account and click OK.

39. Click OK.

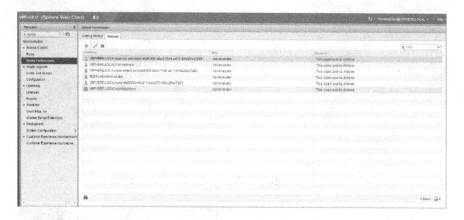

You can now see your administrator account in the list with the role you chose.

40. Click the House Icon with the 4 bars next to it at the top and then click Home.

Configuring Hosts and Clusters

You should be back at the home screen for the vCenter Web Client.

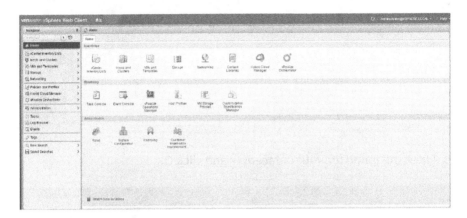

1. Click Hosts and Clusters.

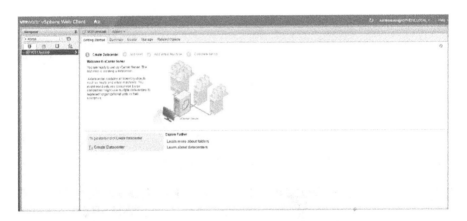

2. Click Create Datacenter in the Getting Started pane.

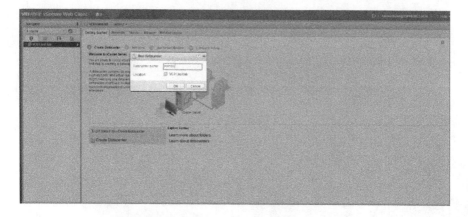

3. Enter the name for your datacenter and click OK.

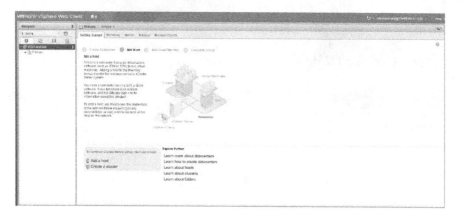

4. Click Create a cluster in the Getting Started pane.

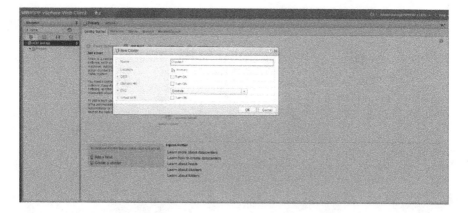

5. Enter a name for the cluster. Do not select any other options at this time and click OK.

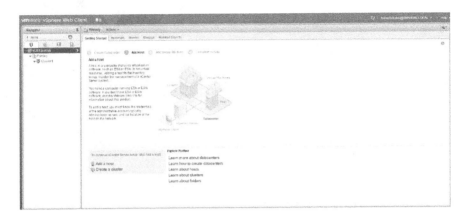

6. Click Add a host.

7. Enter the FQDN (preferable) or IP address of the host that you installed and click Next.

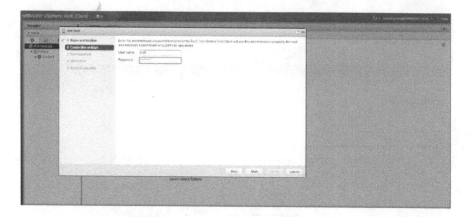

8. Enter the root username and password for the host you are connecting to and click Next.

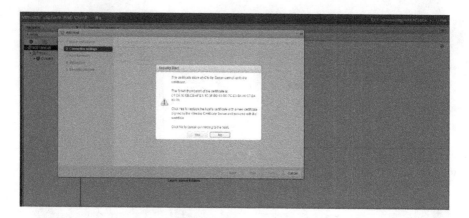

9. Click Yes to accept the self-signed security certificate.

10. Review the summary for the host and click Next.

11. Select the radio button for the license you added in vCenter earlier and click Next.

12. Leave the defaults for the lockdown and click Next.

13. Leave the defaults and click Next.

14. Review the ready to complete page and click Finish.

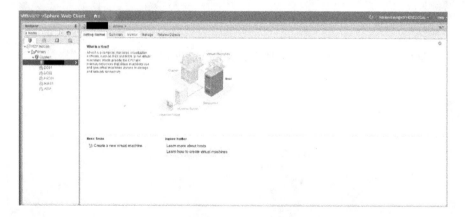

This is what your host will look like when it has been successfully added into vCenter.

15. Click the House/Home icon at the top.

Configuring Storage

In this section, we will be configuring two types of storage (Fibre Channel and NFS), a datastore cluster and a content library; These are the main types of storage you will be working with. iSCSI LUNs show up just like Fibre Channel LUNs do so this process would be the same for those.

Configure a Fibre Channel LUN Datastore

1. From the vCenter Web Client home page, click the Cylinder looking tab.

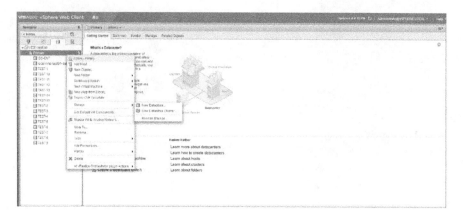

2. Right click on the datacenter then go to Storage then New Datastore.

3. Click Next.

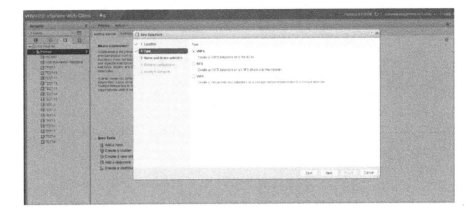

4. Select the radio button for VMFS and click Next.

5. Enter a name for the datastore.

6. Use the drop down box to select the host and select the available LUN and click Next.

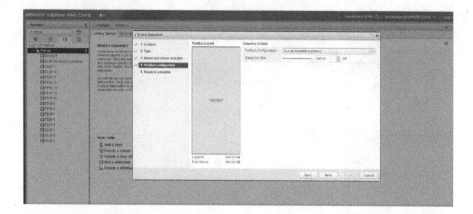

7. Leave the defaults and click Next.

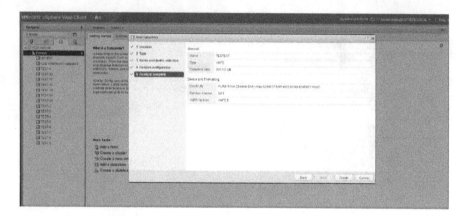

8. Review the information for accuracy and click Next.

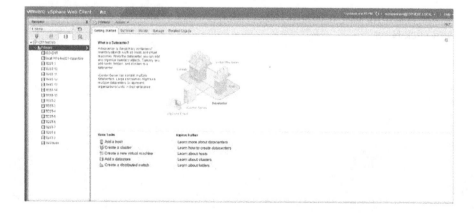

The host will process the request to add the datastore and then you will see it populated in the list.

Configure a NFS Datastore

1. From the vCenter Web Client home page, click the Cylinder looking tab.

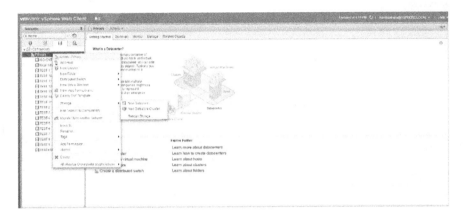

2. Right click on the datacenter then go to Storage then New Datastore.

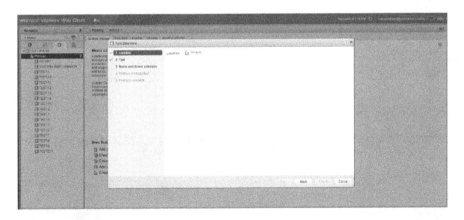

3. Click Next.

4. Select the radio button for NFS and click Next.

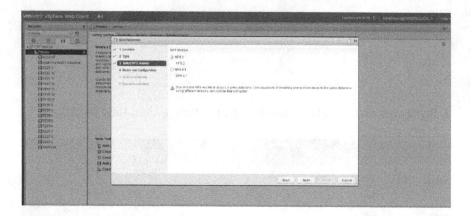

5. Select the radio button for the appropriate NFS version and click Next.

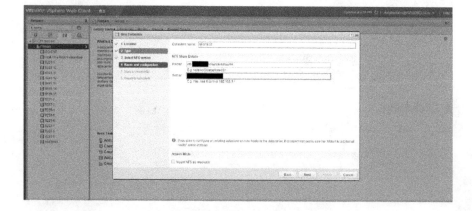

6. Enter a name for the datastore.

7. Enter the complete folder path for the NFS export. (i.e.
/disk/folder1/folder2/nfsshare

8. Enter the FQDN for the NFS server and click Next.

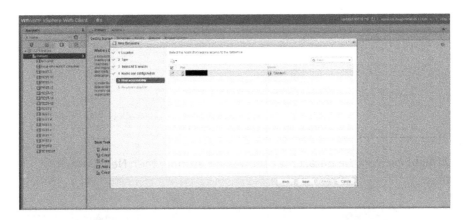

9. Select the hosts you want to access this datastore and click Next.

10. Review the information and click Finish.

You will see the datastore populate after the host has processed the
request. If you receive any errors, make sure you have correctly
configured the NFS server/export and entered the correct information.

Configure a Datastore Cluster

1. From the vCenter Web Client home page, click the Cylinder looking tab.

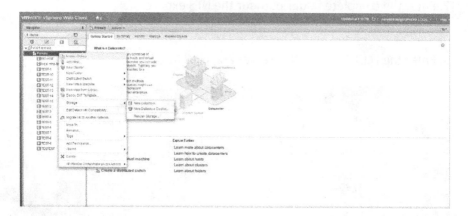

2. Right click on the datacenter then go to Storage then New Datastore Cluster.

3. Enter a name for the datastore cluster, check the box for Storage DRS and click Next.

4. Select the radio button for Fully Automated, leave the defaults and click Next.

5. Check the box for Enable I/O metric for SDRS.

6. Set your acceptable Utilized Space and I/O latency for the storage array and click Next.

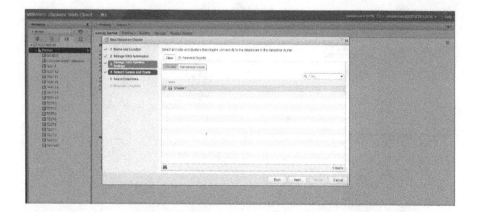

7. Select the cluster to have access to this datastore cluster and click Next.

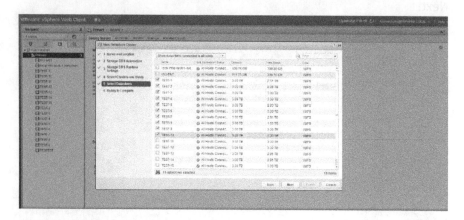

8. Select the datastores that you wish to add to the datastore cluster and click Next.

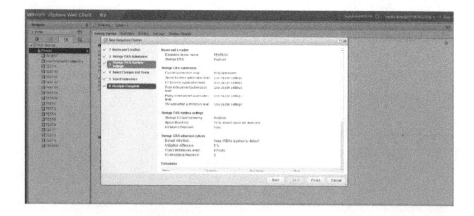

9. Review the information and click Finish.

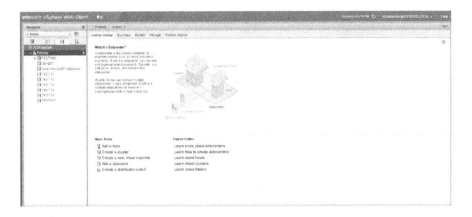

You will see a datastore cluster now and you can click the triangle to expand it and see the individual datastores.

Configure a Content Library

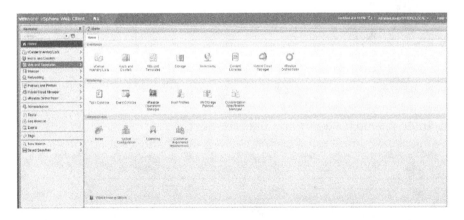

1. Click Content Libraries in the right pane.

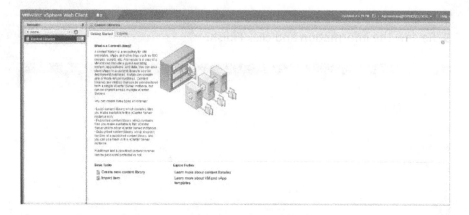

2. Click Create new content library.

3. Enter a name for the library and click Next.

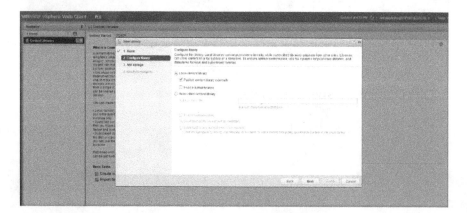

4. Select the radio button for Local content library and check the box for publish content library externally.

5. Select the radio button for Select a datastore and select a datastore then click Next.

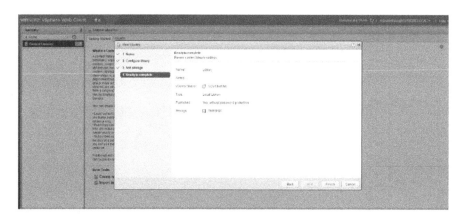

6. Click Finish.

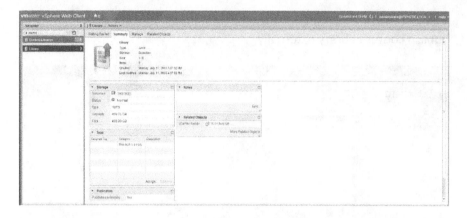

7. Select the library you created to review it.

Congrats! You have just created your first content library. You can store virtual machine templates and ISOs in these. We will talk about that later.

Configuring Networking

Configure a new Virtual Distributed Switch

1. Click the button like looks like Earth in the left pane.

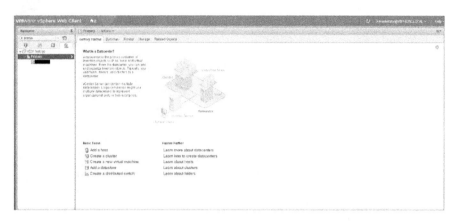

2. Click Create a distributed switch.

3. Enter a name for the switch and click Next.

4. Select the radio button for Distributed Switch 6.0.0 and click Next.

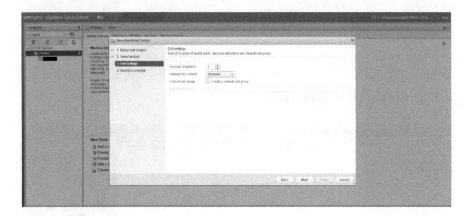

5. Set the number of uplinks that your physical hosts have. (Mine have two.)

6. Use the drop down box and select Enable for Network I/O Control.

7. Uncheck Create a default port group and click Next.

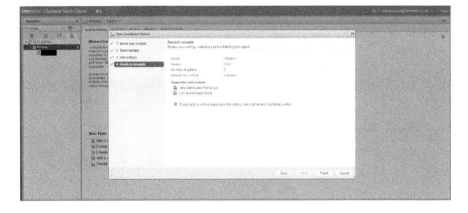

8. Review the information and click Finish.

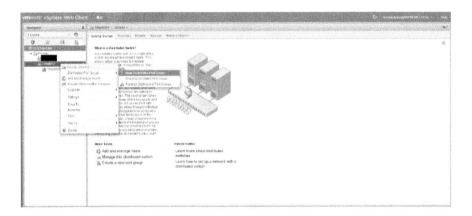

9. Right click the new switch and select Distributed Port Group then New Distributed Port Group.

10. Enter a name for the port group that is descriptive to its function and click Next.

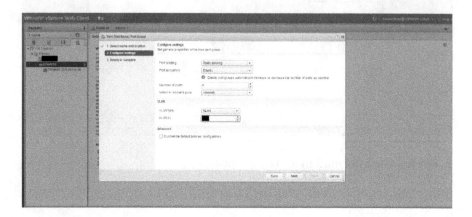

11. Use the drop down boxes to select Static Binding and Elastic. (These should be default.)

12. Use the drop down box to select VLAN enter the VLAN ID and click Next.

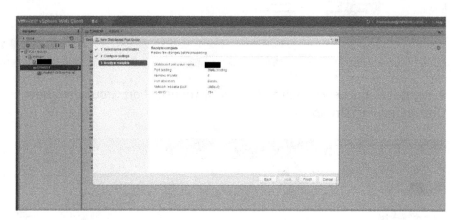

13. Review the information and click Finish.

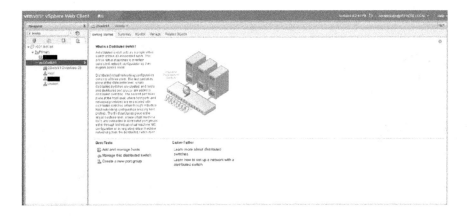

You should now see your port group available. Repeat these steps to add all of the port groups that you need.

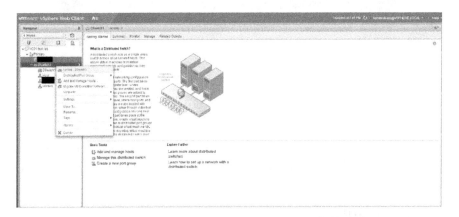

Now we will add a host to the switch.

14. Right click the Distributed Switch and click Add and Manage Hosts.

15. Select the radio button for Add hosts and click Next.

16. Click + New Hosts.

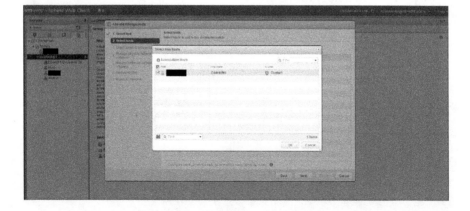

17. Select the host you want to add and click OK.

18. Verify the host and click Next.

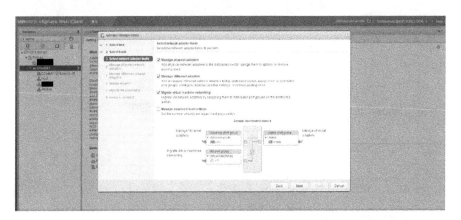

19. Check the boxes for Manage Physical Adapters, Manage VMKernel Adapters and Migrate Virtual Machine Networking then click Next.

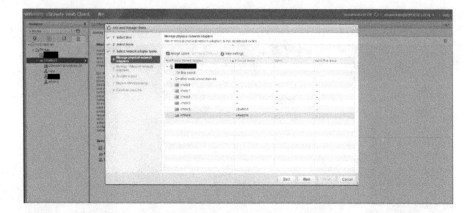

20. Select one of the adapters connected to vSwitch0 and click Assign
Uplink.

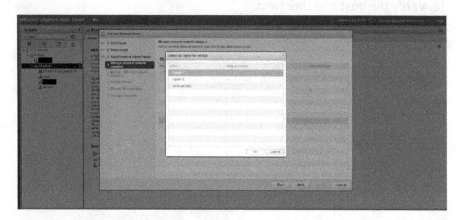

21. Select Uplink 1 and click OK.

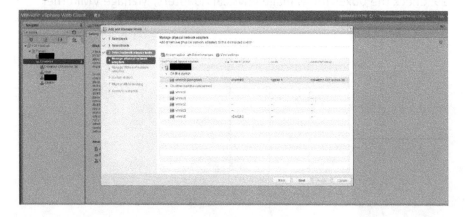

22. Verify the uplink was assigned and click Next.

Do not assign both uplinks yet because an interruption in service is completely likely.

23. Select vmk0 and click Assign Port Group.

24. Select the Port Group you created for the Host Management and click OK.

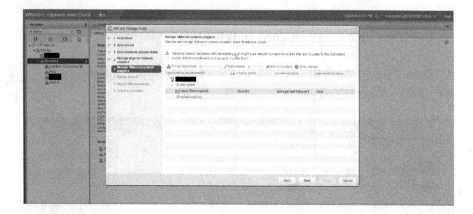

25. Click Next.

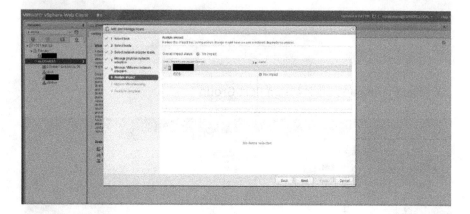

26. Verify there is no impact and click Next.

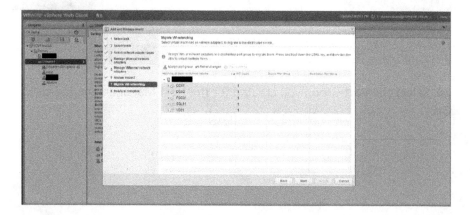

27. Select the virtual machines and click Assign Port Group.

28. Select the Port Group that you created for Virtual Machine traffic and click OK.

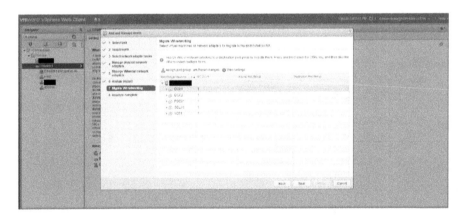

29. Click Next.

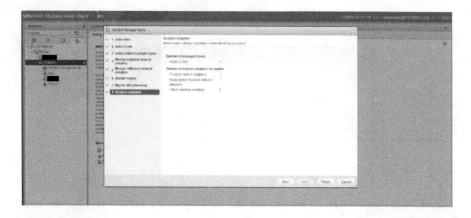

30. Click Finish.

The host will process the networking changes for the host and the virtual machines and then you should be good.

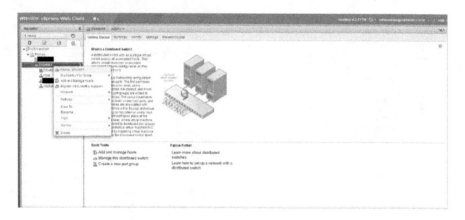

31. Right click on the Distributed Switch and click Add and Manage Hosts.

32. Select the radio button for Manage host networking and click Next.

33. Click + Attached Hosts.

34. Check the box for the host you want to manage and click OK.

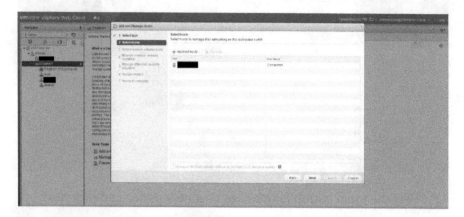

35. Click Next.

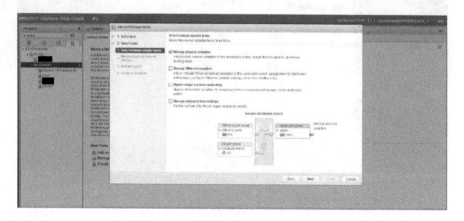

36. Check the box for Manage Physical Adapters and click Next.

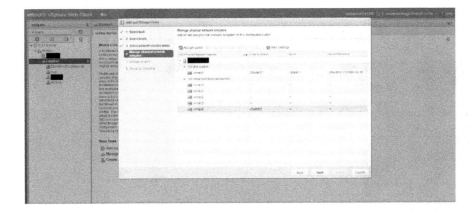

37. Select the physical adapter still connected to vSwitch0 and click Assign Uplink.

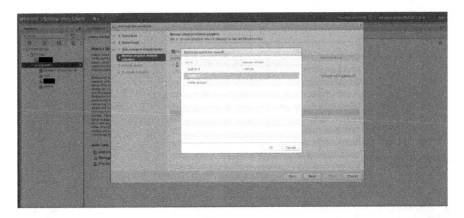

38. Select the Uplink that does not have a physical adapter and click OK.

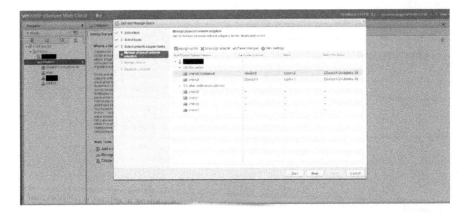

39. Verify the uplink and click Next.

40. Verify there is no impact and click Next.

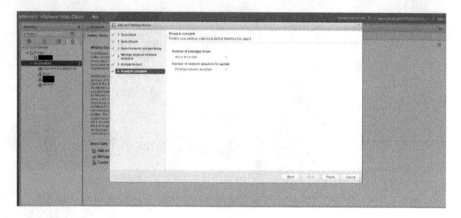

41. Verify the information and click Finish.

42. Click the Switch Uplink Port group.

43. Verify that both of the uplinks are configured correctly.

Your new virtual distributed switch is now configured for use!

Configuring Host Management

Adding More Hosts to the Cluster

1. Click the Host tab on the left pane.

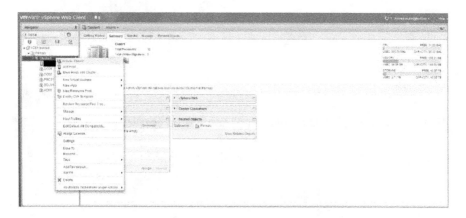

2. Right click on the Cluster and click Add Host.

3. Enter the FQDN or the IP address of the host you want to add and click Next.

4. Enter the root username and password for the host and click Next.

5. Click Yes to accept the self-signed security certificate for the host.

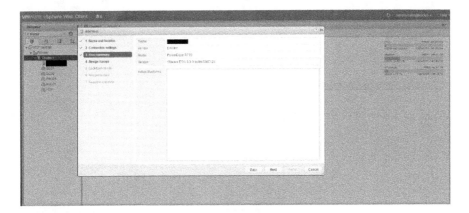

6. Click Next.

7. Select the radio button for the license you want to use and click Next.

8. Select the radio button for Disabled setting for Lockdown Mode and click Next.

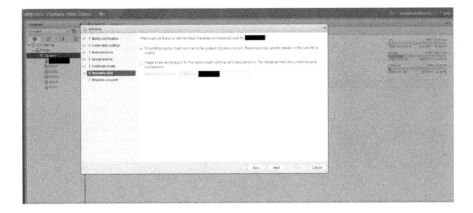

9. Leave the defaults and click Next.

10. Review the information and click Finish.

Repeat these steps to add all of the hosts to the cluster.

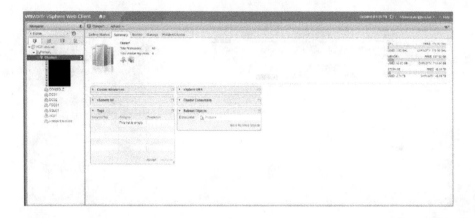

Your cluster should look similar to this. Now that this is complete, you will want to go and add them to the virtual Distributed Switch just like you did for the first host. Please complete that before moving on.

Adding a VMkernel Adapter for vMotion

The next thing we need to do is enable vMotion because it is disabled by default. For this, we will need to add a new VMkernel adapter.

1. Select a host that needs to be configured and click Manage in the right pane.

2. Select Networking and then select VMkernel adapters.

3. Click the Earth looking button.

4. Select the radio button for VMkernel Network Adapter and click Next.

5. Select the radio button for Select an existing network and click Browse.

6. Select the Port Group that you created for vMotion and click OK.

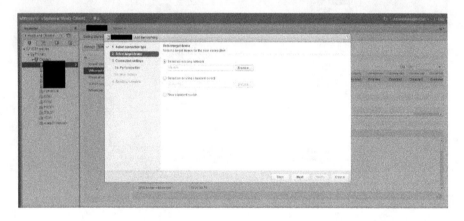

7. Verify the proper Port Group was selected and click Next.

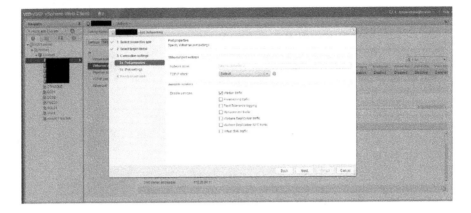

8. Check the box for vMotion traffic and click Next.

9. Select the use static IPv4 setting and enter the IP for this adapter and click Next.

I always use the same last octet for my host management IP and my vMotion IP on different VLANs.

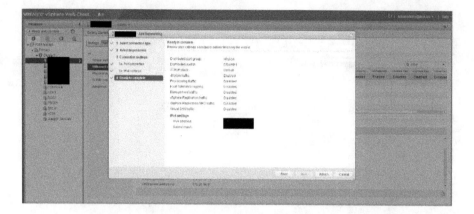

10. Review the information and click Finish.

You should now see two VMkernel adapters on your host.

Creating, Applying, and Remediating a Host Profile

In this section, we will create a host profile. These are super handy for making sure that your hosts have the same configurations and you can go pretty granular with them. We will be creating a profile specifically for NTP settings. These host profiles can be compared to Windows Group Policies.

1. Front the vCenter Web Client home screen, click Host Profiles in the right pane.

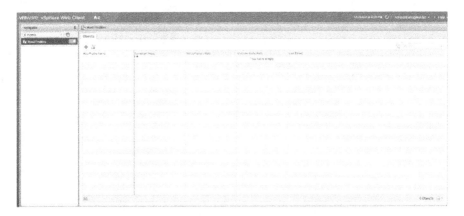

2. Click the green +.

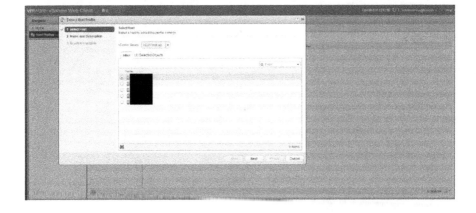

3. Select the radio button for a host you want to use for a reference and click Next.

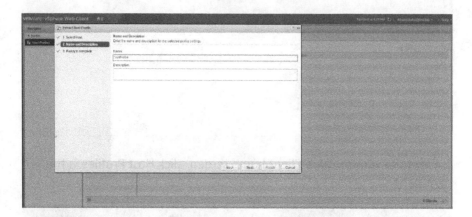

4. Enter a name and description for the profile and click Next.

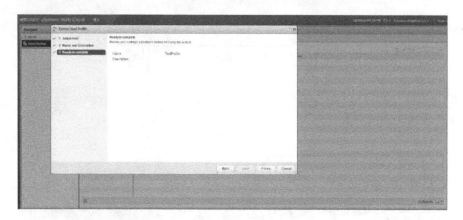

5. Review the information and click Finish.

Once the reference information has been pulled from the host, you will need your new profile.

6. Select the profile.

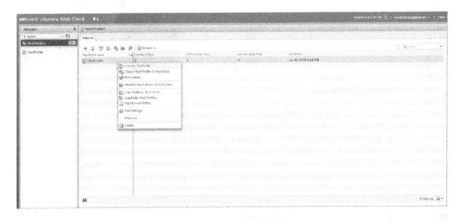

7. Click Actions then Edit Settings.

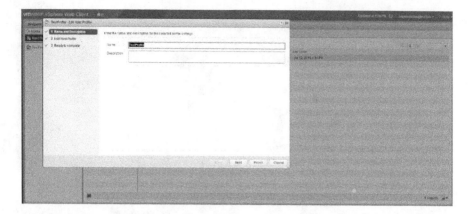

8. Click Next.

9. You will want to uncheck everything but the following setting:

General System Settings > Date and Time Configuration

10. Select Date and Time Configuration item under General System Settings > Date and Time Configuration.

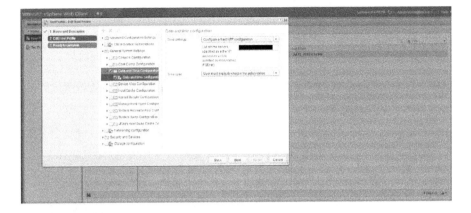

11. Use the drop down box to select Configure a fixed NTP configuration, enter your NTP servers and click Next.

12. Review the information and click Finish.

13. Select the profile, click Actions then click Attach/Detach Hosts and Clusters.

14. Select the cluster you want to attach, click Attach then click Next.

15. Click Finish.

16. Select the profile, click Actions then click Check Host Profile Compliance.

You will then see how many compliant/non-compliant/unknown hosts you have. If you have unknown hosts, you may need to put them in maintenance mode and reboot them before trying to remediate the host profile.

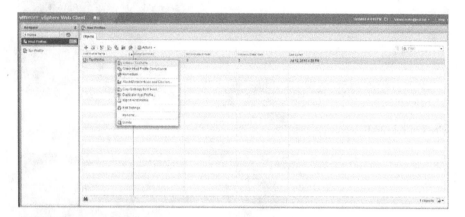

17. Select the profile, click Actions then click Remediate.

18. Check the box for the cluster you want to remediate and click Next.

19. Click Next.

20. Review the hosts that will be remediated and click Finish.

After the task completes, I can see that all of my hosts are now compliant with the NTP host profile we created.

Configuring Availability

In this section, we will do a basic configuration of HA and DRS to get it enabled on our clusters.

Configuring DRS and HA

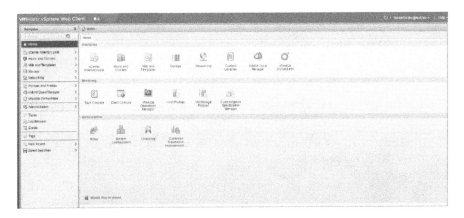

1. On the vCenter Web Client home page, click the Host and Clusters tab.

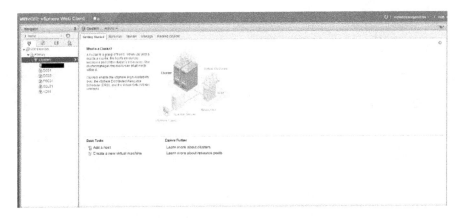

2. Select the cluster and click the Manage tab in the right pane.

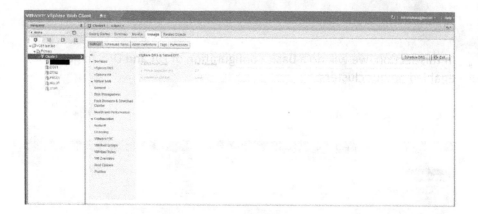

3. Click the Settings tab then select vSphere DRS and click the Edit button.

4. Check the box to enable DRS.

5. Use the drop down menu to select Fully Automated and select Off for Power Management.

6. Expand the DRS Automation section by clicking on the triangle.

7. Leave the defaults and click OK.

Once the task has been finished, DRS will be enabled for your cluster.

8. Select vSphere HA.

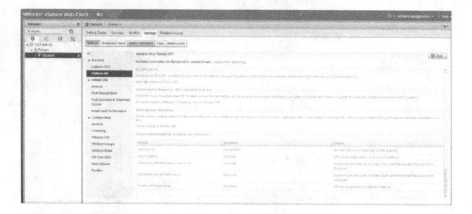

9. Click Edit.

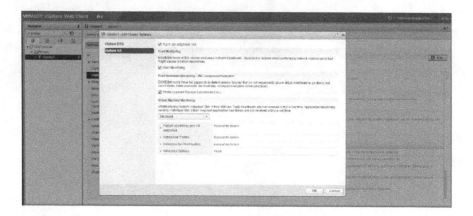

10. Check the box to enable HA.

11. Check the box for Host Monitoring and Protect against Storage Connectivity Loss.

12. Click the triangle to expand the Admission Control section.

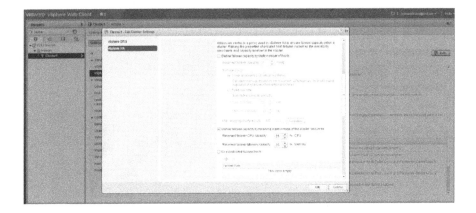

There are four different ways to allocate resources for HA. The least complex and easiest to manage is the Percentage of Resources per host.

13. Select the radio button for Define failover capacity by reserving a percentage of cluster resources.

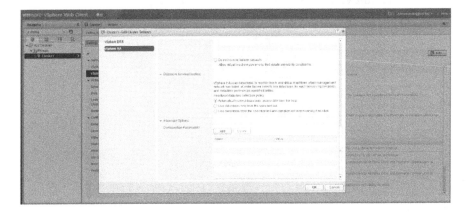

14. Click the triangle to expand the Datastore for Heartbeating section.

15. Select the radio button for automatically select datastores accessible from the host.

16. Click OK.

Once the task completes, you will have a completely HA/DRS enabled cluster. Now this is just a basic configuration and depending on your resource loads and failure requirements, you may configuration this in a completely different fashion. This is the least complex solution to get up and running. You should evaluate this over time to make sure that it continues to suit your needs and adjust as necessary.

Configuring Virtual Machine Management

Create a Guest Customization Specification

1. From the vCenter Web Client home page, click Customization Specification Manager.

2. Click the page with a +.

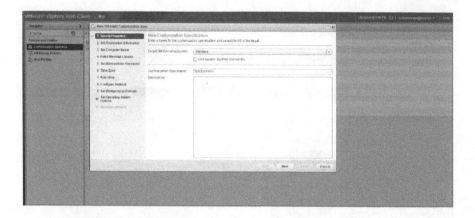

3. Use the drop down box to choose Windows for the OS, enter a name for the specification and click Next.

I usually name them based on domain or workgroup and sometimes function.

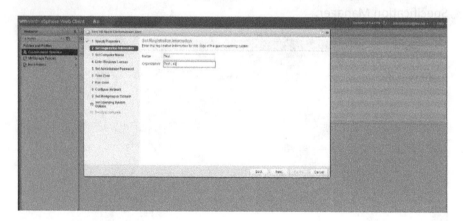

4. Enter a name and organization then click Next.

5. Select the radio button for Use the virtual machine name and click Next.

6. Left the defaults on this screen and click Next.

I do my activations by using the volume license tools with AD activation. If you create a spec for a workgroup, go ahead and put in your MAK or KMS key here.

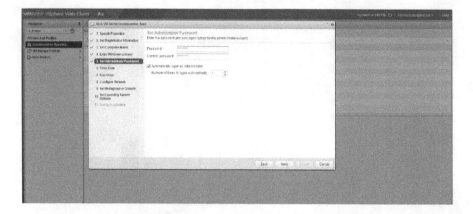

7. Enter an administrator password and select the number of times it should auto logon then click Next.

8. Use the drop down box to select the correct time zone and click Next.

9. Leave the defaults on this screen and click Next.

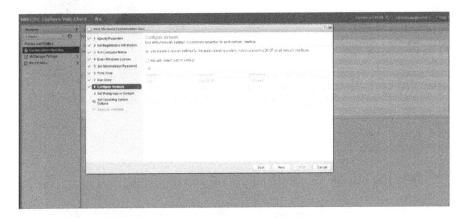

10. Leave the defaults on this screen and click Next.

You can select manual and choose the option to prompt for a static IP every time you deploy if you want.

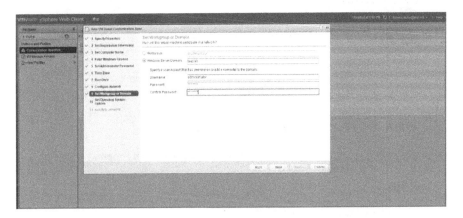

11. Select the radio button for workgroup or domain, fill out the appropriate information and click Next.

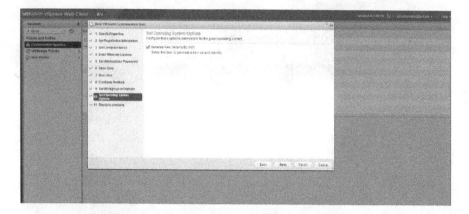

12. Check the box for Generate a new SID and click Next.

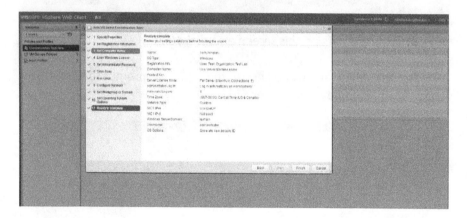

13. Review the information and click Finish.

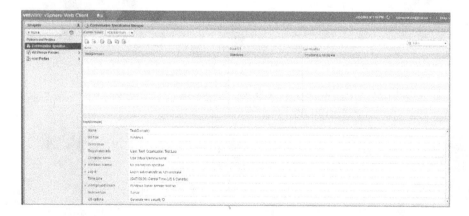

Now you have completed your first guest customization specification. If you want to create some more, you can do that before moving on.

Create a Virtual Machine Template

In this section, you will go back to the previous section for deploying virtual machines. I don't really want to rehash that (fluff policy). Once you have deployed a brand new virtual machine, go ahead and shut it down and continue.

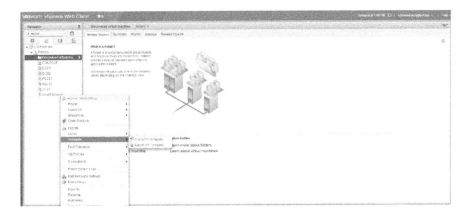

1. In the Virtual Machines and Templates tab, right click on your virtual machine and select Template > Convert to Template.

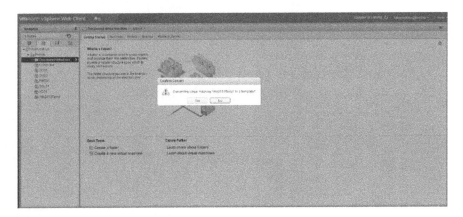

2. Click on Yes.

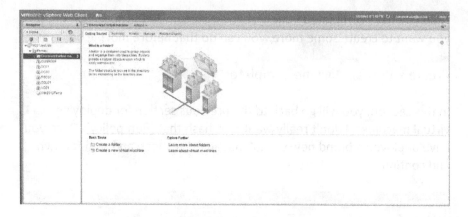

Now you have a template created! Pretty simple.

Deploy a Virtual Machine from a Template

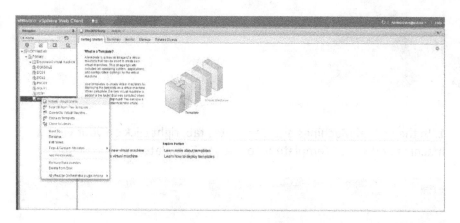

1. In the Virtual Machines and Templates tab, right click on your virtual machine template and click New VM from this Template.

2. Enter a name for the virtual machine, select the datacenter to deploy to then click Next.

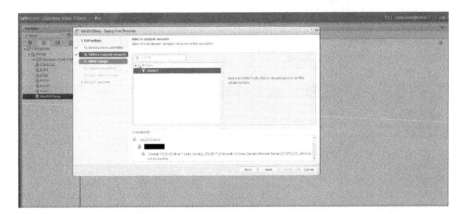

3. Select a cluster to deploy to and click Next.

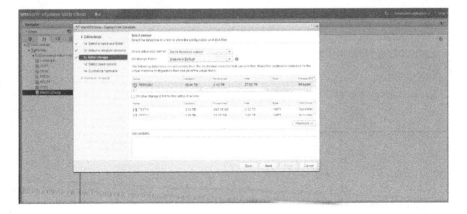

4. Select the datastore cluster/datastore to store the virtual machine in and click Next.

5. Check the boxes for customize the operating system and power on after creation and click Next.

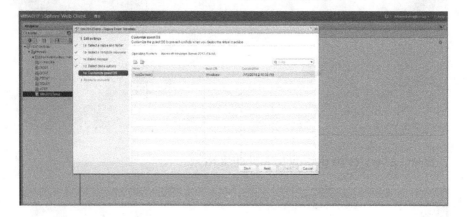

6. Select the customization that you created and click Next.

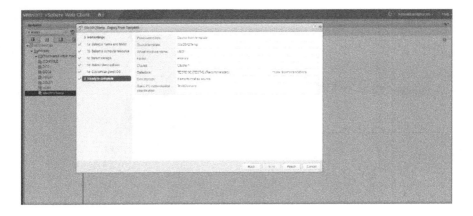

7. Review the information and click Finish.

The task will first deploy the VM to storage and then power it on. vCenter creates a scheduled task to run the customization so it could take up to 5 minutes to start. Go grab some coffee or a snack and come back to check it.

Clone a Virtual Machine Template to a Content Library

Now we are back to the content library. Content libraries are the newest and hottest thing for templates and ISOs. Here we will clone our new template to the content library.

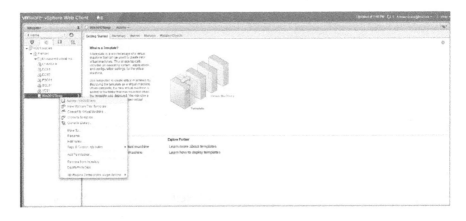

1. Right click on the template, click Clone to Library.

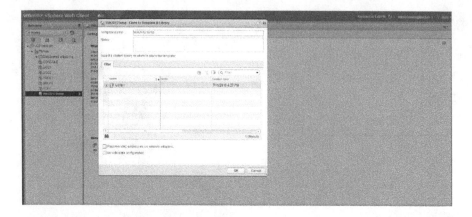

2. Enter a name for the template, select the content library and click OK.

That's it! Done deal. Once the template has been uploaded to the content library, you can proceed to the next section.

Deploy a Virtual Machine from a Template in a Content Library

1. From the vCenter Web Client home page, click Content Libraries.

2. Click Related Objects.

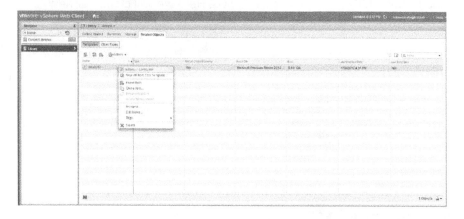

3. Select the temple, click Actions then click New VM from this template.

4. Enter a name for this VM, select the datacenter then click Next.

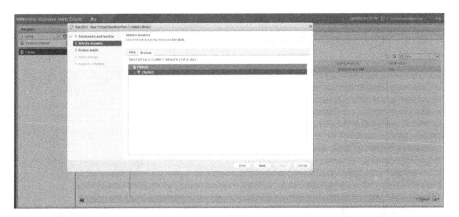

5. Select the cluster and click Next.

6. Review the details and click Next.

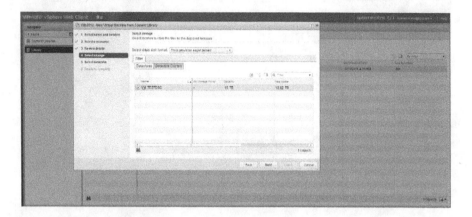

7. Click the Datastore Clusters tab and select the radio button for your Datastore Cluster then click Next.

8. Select the Port Group that you want the VM on and click Next.

9. Review the details and click Finish.

So you may have noticed that you didn't get an option to customize like you did with the normal template. When we deploy from a content library, we have to manually customize it.

10. Click on the Virtual Machines and Templates tab.

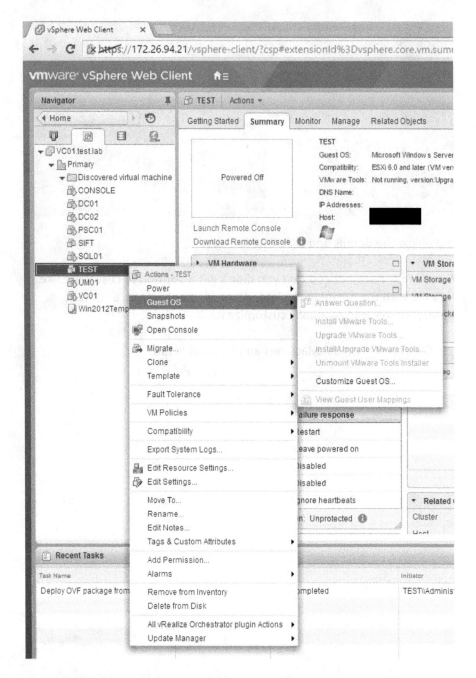

11. Right click on the powered off virtual machine and select Guest OS > Customize Guest OS.

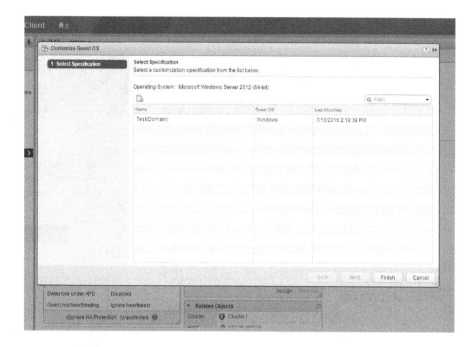

12. Select the customization specification that you want to use and click Finish.

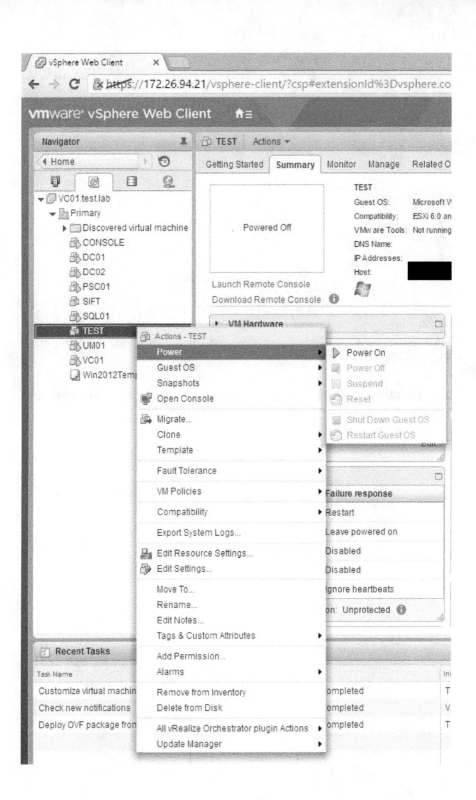

13. Right click on the virtual machine and select Power > Power On.

Now your guest will customize!

Installing and Configuring Update Manager

In this section, we will be deploying and configuring vSphere Update Manager. We will also create a baseline, scan and remediate our cluster.

I downloaded the OpenManage Server Assistant from Dell so I can install it as part of this section. You may or may not need to do this depending on the customized ISO you downloaded to install ESXi and how out of date it might be.

1. Deploy a new virtual machine to the cluster for Update Manager.

This can coexist with vCenter for Windows, but you will need another VM for the vCenter Server Appliance.

2. After the VM has deployed, Login and copy the vCenter media to the VM.

3. Add a new drive to the VM and format it properly for Windows. This should be at least 120GB.

4. Mount the ISO and run the Autorun.

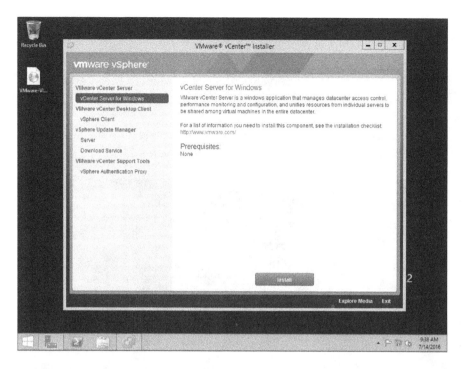

5. Select Server under vSphere Update Manager.

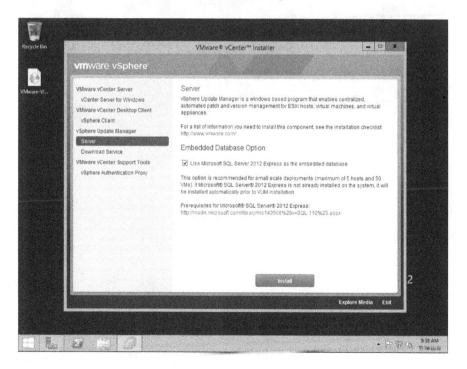

6. Leave the defaults and click Install.

You can either use SQL Server Express or connect to the vCenter for Windows SQL Server and create a database there.

Do not use SQL Server Express if you are installing it on the vCenter for Windows VM or you will have performance problems.

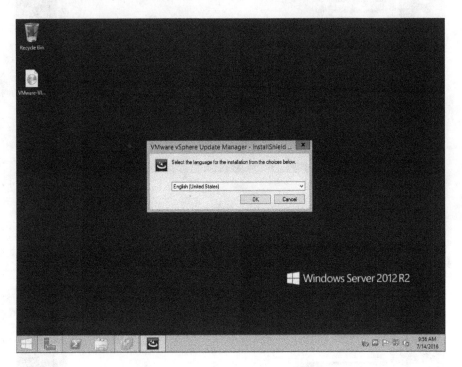

7. Click OK.

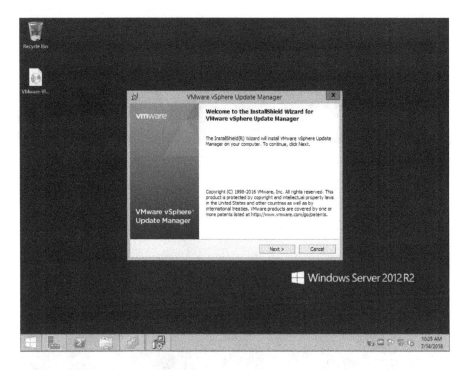

8. Click Next.

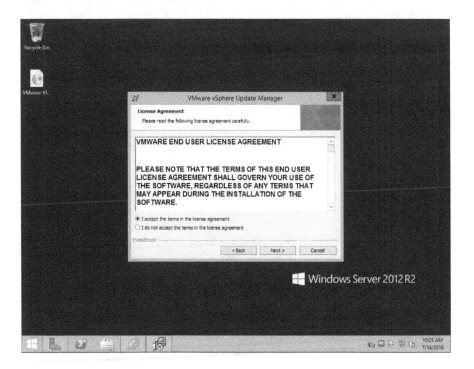

9. Select the radio button for I accept and click Next.

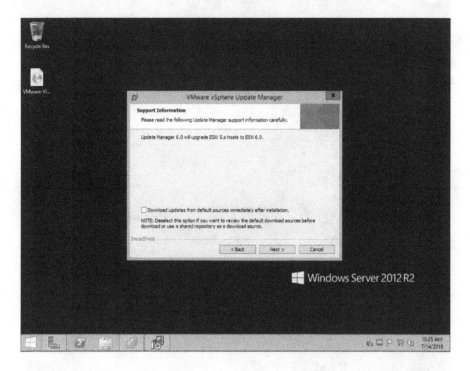

10. Uncheck the box for Download updates immediately after installation and click Next.

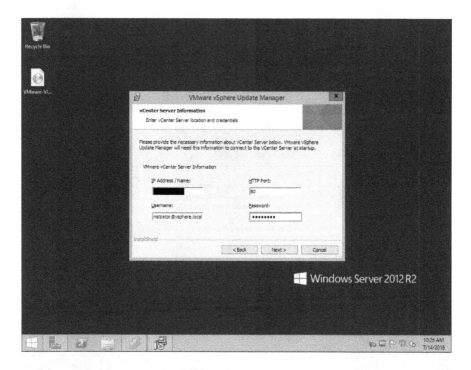

11. Enter the information applicable to your vCenter server and click Next.

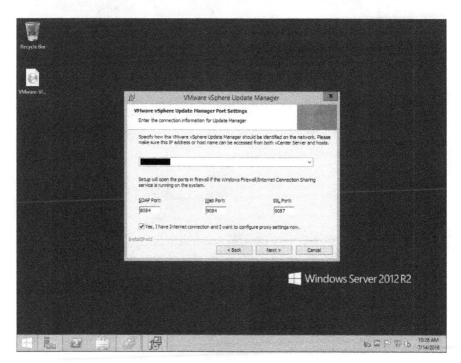

12. Check the box for Yes, I have Internet connection and I want to configure a proxy and click Next.

Do this only if you have a proxy.

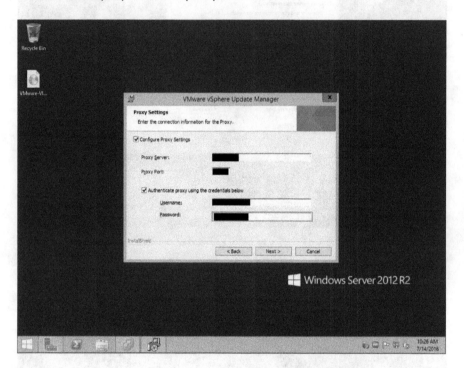

13. Enter the information for your proxy server and click Next.

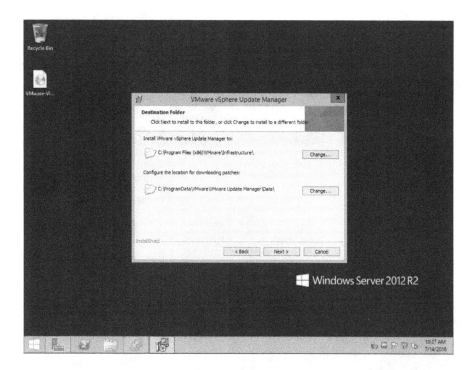

14. Click Browse for the Configure the location for downloading patches.

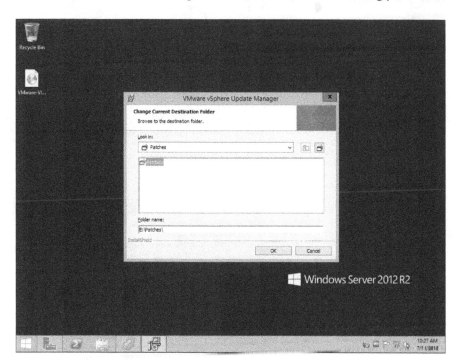

15. Create a folder on the extra drive and browse to it then click Next.

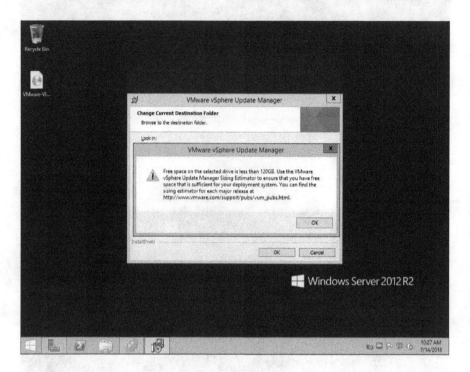

16. If you did not create a 120GB+ drive, you will receive this message.
Click OK.

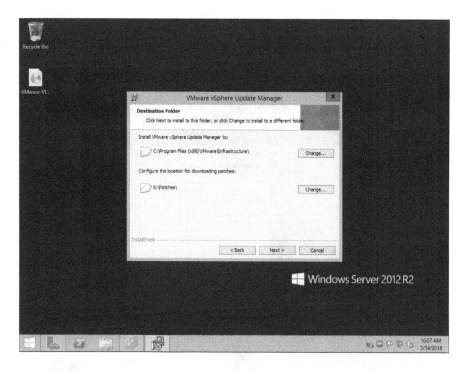

17. Click Next.

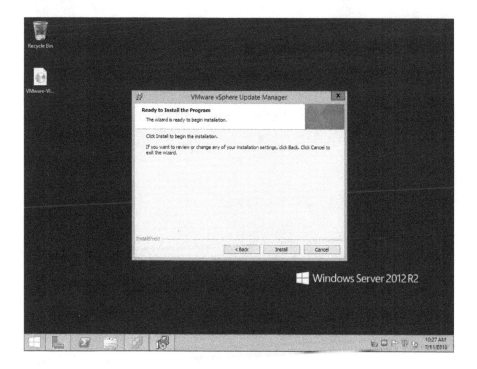

18. Click Install.

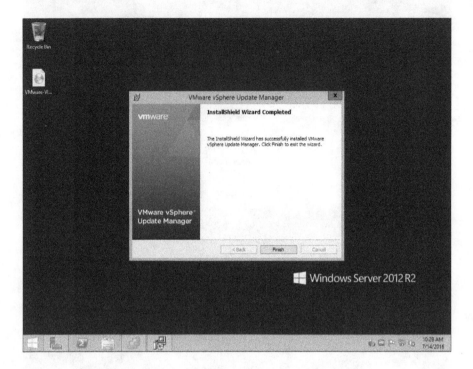

19. Click Finish.

Update Manager is now successfully installed.

20. Open the vSphere client (Not the web client) and connect to the vCenter server.

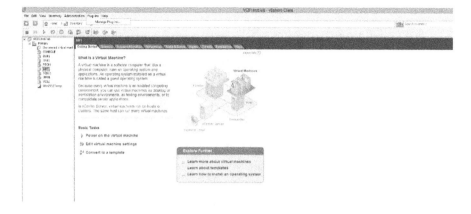

21. Click the Plug-ins menu and Click Manage Plug-ins.

22. Scroll down and click the blue link for Download and Install next to vSphere Update Manager.

23. Click Run if prompted.

24. Click OK.

25. Click Next.

26. Select the radio button for I accept and Click Next.

27. Click Install.

28. Click Finish.

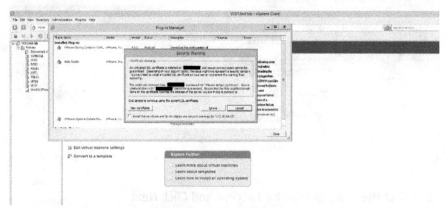

29. The plug-in will activate and click Ignore to continue.

30. Click Close.

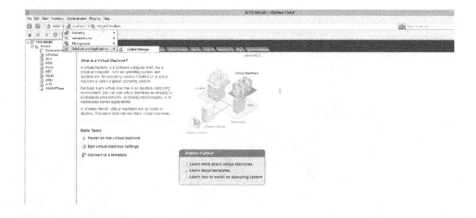

31. Click Inventory > Solutions and Applications > Update Manager.

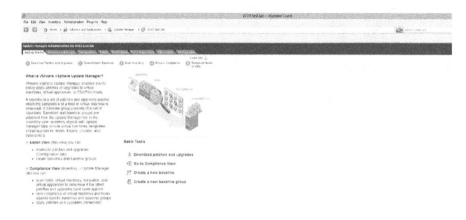

32. Click Baselines and Groups.

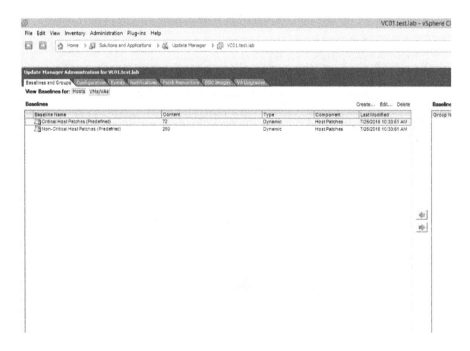

33. Click Patch Repository.

34. Click Import Patches

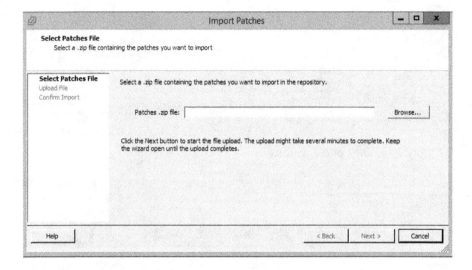

35. Click Browse and find the file you downloaded and select it.

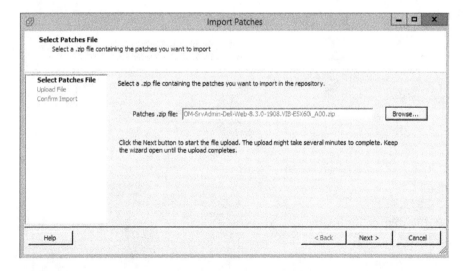

36. Click Next.

37. Click Ignore.

38. Click Finish.

39. Click Baselines and Groups.

40. Click Create.

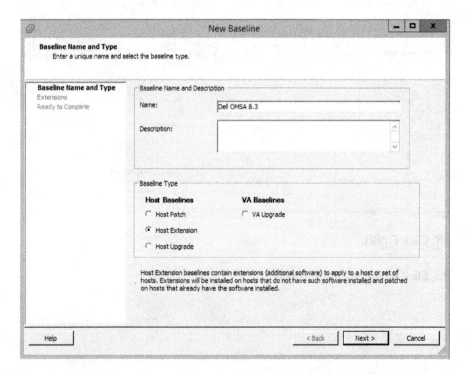

41. Enter a name for the Baseline, select the radio button for Host Extension and click Next.

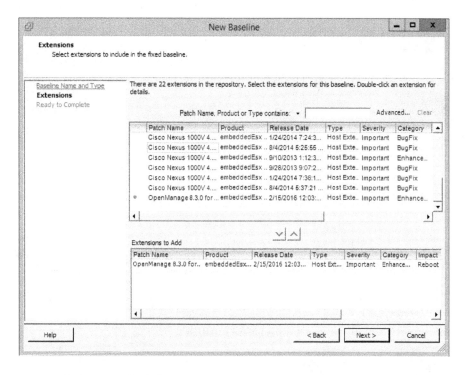

42. Scroll down to find the extension you uploaded, select the extension, click the Down arrow then click Next.

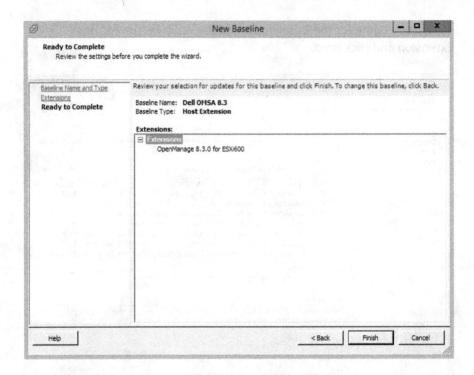

43. Review the information and click Finish.

44. Click Home.

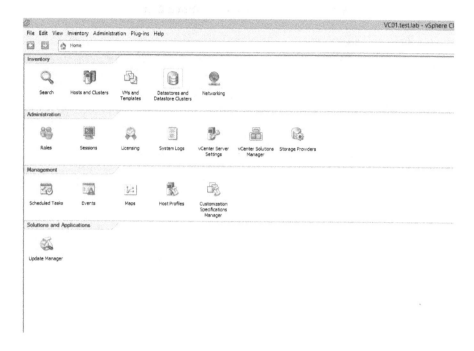

45. Click Hosts and Clusters

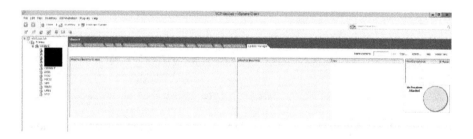

46. Select the Cluster and click the Update Manager Tab.

47. Click Attach.

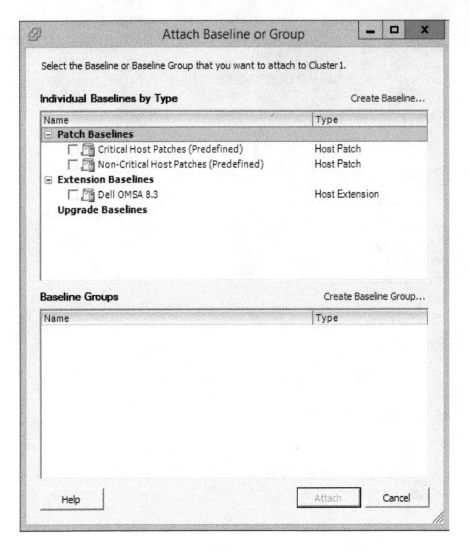

48. Check the boxes for the Critical, Non-Critical, and Extension baselines and click Attach.

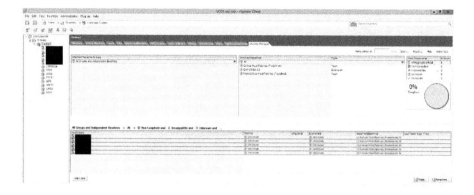

49. Click Scan.

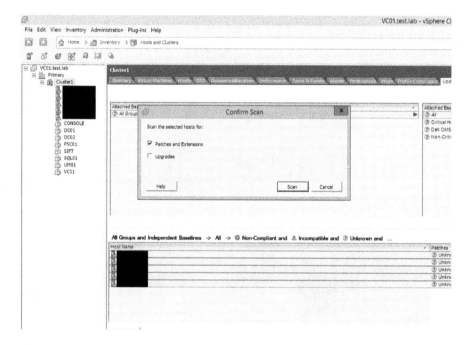

50. Uncheck Upgrades and click Scan.

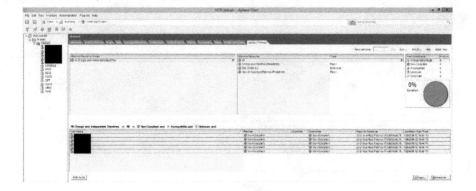

After the scan has completed, you will see that your cluster is not compliant.

51. Click Stage.

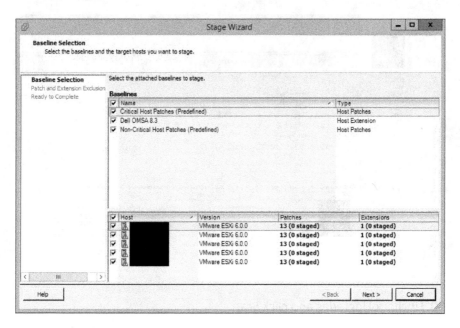

52. Select all of the baselines for staging and click Next.

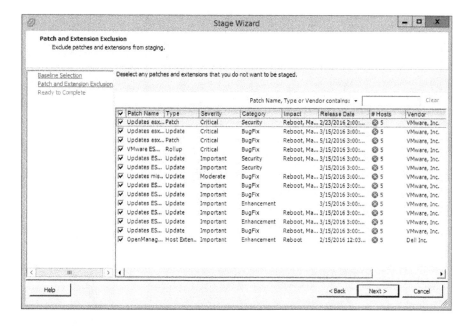

53. All of the patches should be selected. Click Next.

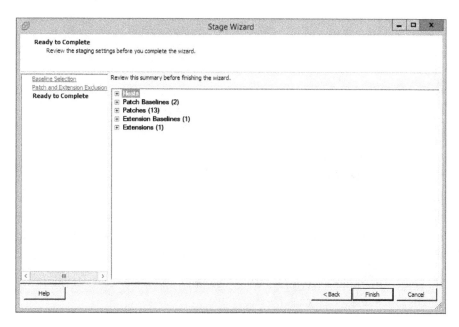

54. Click Finish.

In the Tasks window you will see the staging begin.

Here you can see the staging tasks complete.

55. Click Remediate.

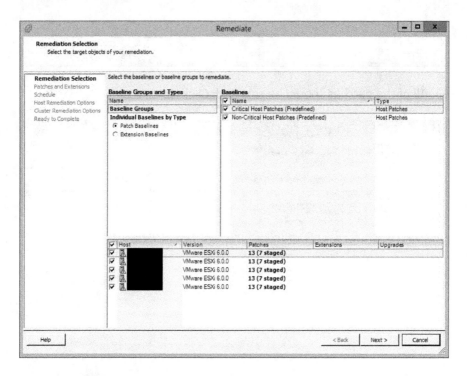

56. Select the radio button for Patch Baselines and check both of the patches baselines then click Next.

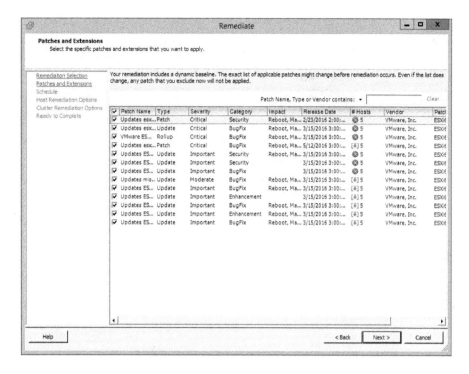

57. Review the patches and click Next.

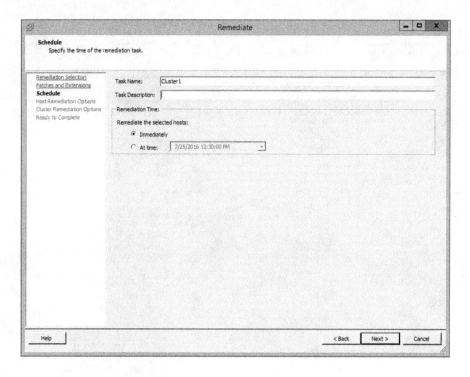

58. Enter a name for the task and select the radio button for Immediately then click Next.

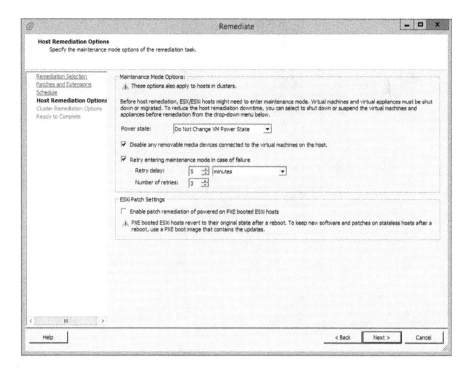

59. Check the box for Disable any removable media devices and click Next.

If you don't check this box then it could hold the host in waiting for maintenance mode.

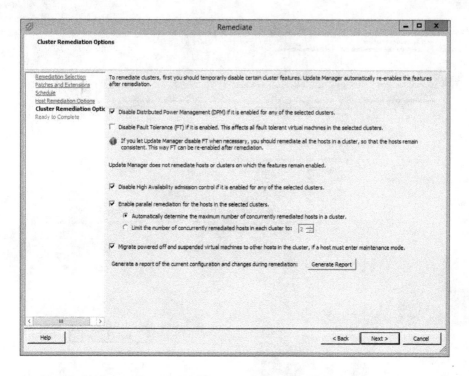

60. Check the boxes for Disable High Availability, Enable parallel remediation (Select Automatically), and Migrate Powered off and suspended then click Next.

If you don't check these boxes then it could hold the host in waiting for maintenance mode.

Depending on the cluster I will choose Automatic or set the number myself of the parallel remediation. vSphere can go crazy sometimes so just test it out.

I have seen some issues with VMs losing their network card settings in Windows if they are not migrated when a host is patched. Its pretty weird, but I can replicate it. Just choose this option to be safe.

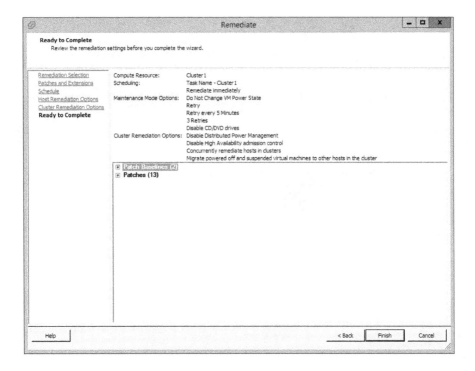

61. Click Finish.

If you watch the Tasks window, you will see hosts vMotioning VMs and going into Maintenance mode.

You will see installs happening.

Then you will see reboots being initiated. Once those tasks are complete

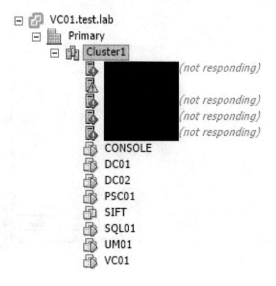

Once those tasks are complete, you will see vCenter lose connections to the hosts.

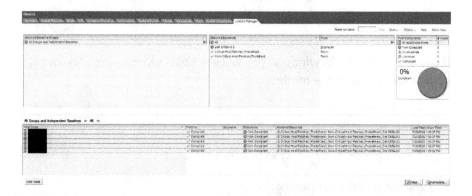

Once the hosts come back up, you will see the patches are now compliant. If it doesn't show automatically, you will need to do a rescan.

62. Click Remediate.

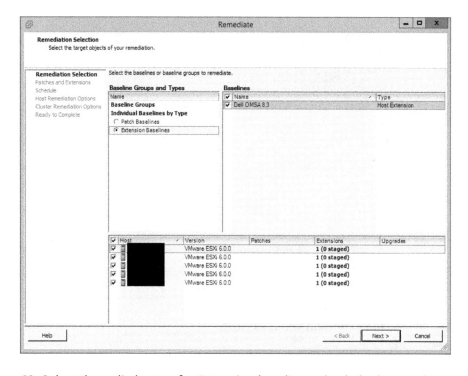

63. Select the radio button for Extension baselines, check the box, and click Next.

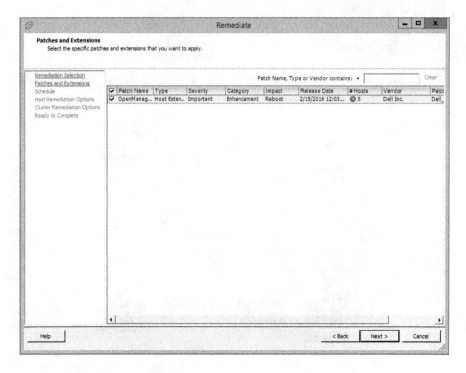

64. Review the extension and click Next.

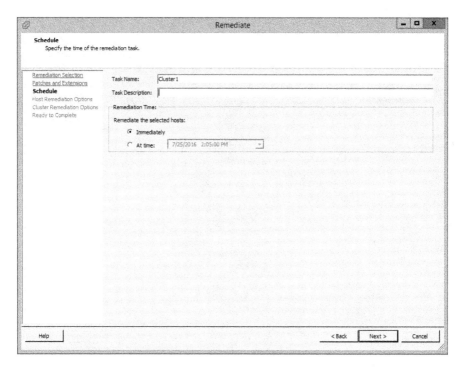

65. Enter a name for the task, select the radio button for Immediately and click Next.

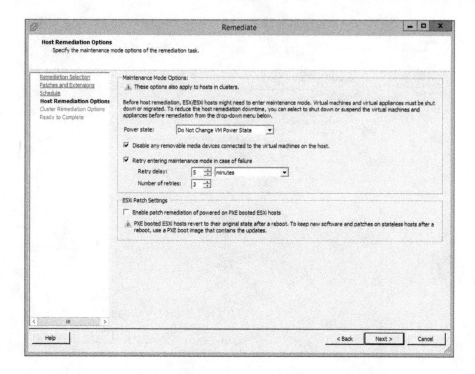

66. Check the disable removable media box and click Next.

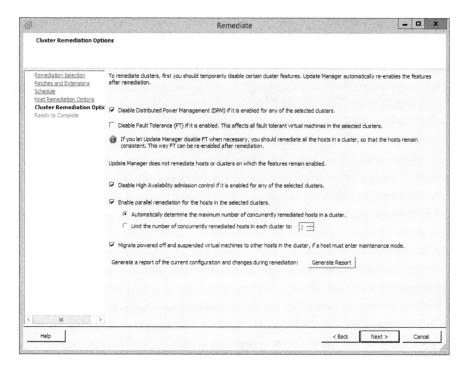

67. Check the Disable HA, Enable Parallel Remediate, and Migrate checkboxes and click Next.

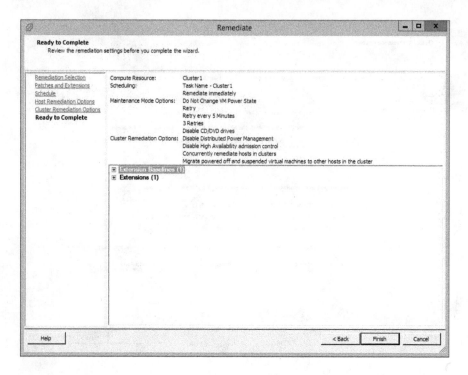

68. Click Finish.

69. Click Scan if your cluster did not come up 100% compliant.

You have successfully added a host extension and completely patched your cluster!

Appendix: External Resources

In this appendix, we a going to list a several places to visit and get some cool toys or read more about that "fluff" that I didn't want to present.

VMWare Hands on Labs: http://labs.hol.vmware.com/

VMware HOL is great and if you don't have a test lab or just want to have an easy environment to build some stuff. It is structured just like classroom lab exercises.

VMWare Documentation: https://www.vmware.com/support/pubs/

VMware's documentation site is extremely extensive and you should definitely be familiar with it. It is hard to dig through and there aren't many real world examples, but they definitely list out pitfalls that will destroy or hold up your implementation. Some stuff in also found the VMware Knowledge Base.

VMWare Flings: https://labs.vmware.com/flings

VMware Flings are really cool toys that you can play with. Some are useful and others are just interesting. Sometimes the really popular flings get adapted into the product like the new HTML5 client.

Duncan Epping: http://www.yellow-bricks.com/
                http://www.yellow-bricks.com/esxtop/
                http://www.yellow-bricks.com/vmware-high-availability-deepdiv/

I follow this guy on twitter and his blog has the singular source of the best information on how HA works. He literally wrote the book and then adapted it to his blog.

Frank Denneman: http://frankdenneman.nl/
                 http://frankdenneman.nl/2016/07/07/numa-deep-dive-part-1-uma-numa/
                 http://frankdenneman.nl/2016/07/08/numa-deep-dive-part-2-system-architecture/

http://frankdenneman.nl/vmotion/

Same with this guy. Follow him.

Rene Van Den Bedem: https://vcdx133.com/

This guy documented his entire journey through the VCDX program and he has a ton of good information.

This last link is to the single most interested and detailed book about IT architecture that I can find. It is written by three VCDXs and if you have any interest in being a VCDX or an IT architect in general, you should buy this book. The knowledge contained is invaluable.

IT Architect: Foundation in the Art of Infrastructure Design: A Practical Guide for IT Architects

https://www.amazon.com/Architect-Foundation-Infrastructure-Practical-Architects/dp/0996647708/ref=sr_1_1?ie=UTF8&qid=1469545789&sr=8-1&keywords=it+architect

There are plenty more I can add, but google or follow these guys. They post links and show the best stuff out there. Sorry if I missed anyone!